journey
TO THE
wild
Heart

Journey
TO THE
wild
Heart

Four Invitations
to Contemplative Living

Amy Frykholm

ORBIS BOOKS
Maryknoll, New York 10545

Published by Orbis Books, Box 302, Maryknoll, NY 10545-0302.

Scripture quotations (unless otherwise noted) are taken from the New American Standard Bible®, copyright © 1960, 1962, 1963, 1968, 1971, 1972, 1973, 1975, 1977, 1995 by The Lockman Foundation. Used by permission (www.Lockman.org).

Manufactured in the United States of America

Library of Congress Cataloging-in-Publication Data
Names: Frykholm, Amy Johnson, 1971- author.
Title: Journey to the wild heart : four invitations to copntemplative
    living / Amy Frykholm.
Description: Maryknoll, NY : Orbis Books, [2025] | Includes bibliographical
    references. | Summary: "Four Invitations to the contemplative spiritual
    life-Discover, Behold, Bewilder, Discern-guide us on a treasure hunt
    through our inner lives"—Provided by publisher.
Identifiers: LCCN 2024037277 (print) | LCCN 2024037278 (ebook) | ISBN
    9781626986053 (trade paperback) | ISBN 9798888660607 (epub)
Subjects: LCSH: Spiritual life—Protestant churches. | Contemplation.
Classification: LCC BV4501.3 .F785 2025 (print) | LCC BV4501.3 (ebook) |
    DDC 248.4—dc23/eng/20240925
LC record available at https://lccn.loc.gov/2024037277
LC ebook record available at https://lccn.loc.gov/2024037278

For Jay,
who told me to speak a word of freedom to people

contents

Foreword   *ix*

Introduction: Into the Journey   *1*

Part I Invitations

Invitation One: Discover   13

Invitation Two: Behold   23

Invitation Three: Bewilder   33

Invitation Four: Discern   43

Part II Sessions

Session One: A Door   55

Session Two: A Time   65

Session Three: A Place   73

Session Four: A Companion   81

Session Five: An In-Between   87

Session Six: An Obstacle   95

Journey to the Wild Heart

Session Seven: A Pause   103

Session Eight: A Maze   107

Session Nine: A Moment   115

Session Ten: A Dragonfly   123

Journeying On   131

Acknowledgments   137

foreword

Carl McColman

In her 1931 poem "The Song of the Highway," civil rights activist (and later in life, Episcopal priest) Pauli Murray subtly evokes what is perhaps the oldest and most enduring metaphor for the spiritual life: a road or a pilgrimage. In the poem, Murray imagines what the highway itself might have to say to us. It calls itself "the spine of the earth," bringing wayfarers and travelers into close encounters with nature, flora and fauna, the ever-changing dynamics of the weather, and the cycle of the seasons.

Sensual and musical, the poem evokes birdsong and lowing cattle and other sounds of the earth that accompany the highway—and those who traverse upon it—over its many miles. But this is a song where music, and sound, do not have the last word. The highway finally declares, "I go on in silence," reminding us that between every song, every story, and indeed each thought or moment of awareness, we may find the vast ocean of limitless silence—what Thomas Keating called "God's first language."

Amy Frykholm knows the sacred song and embodied cadence of the open road; she wrote her luminous meditation on the early desert saint, Mary of Egypt, after a pilgrimage in which she sought to encounter the abiding spirit of that holy woman in her own habitat. Like all thoughtful pilgrims, she understands that a spiritual journey unfolds as much in our pulsing heart as through the pounding of our feet. I first discovered Amy Frykholm's considerable gifts as a writer when I read her "contemplative biography" of Julian of Norwich, the fourteenth century mystic who took her own inner pilgrimage while living in seclusion in a small cell adjacent to a medieval church.

All this reminds me of my favorite word of wisdom from the Irish mystic John O'Donohue, who said, "If there were a spiritual journey, it would be only a quarter inch long, though many miles deep." Take a step back from his wry Celtic humor, though, and consider what this invitation represents. The migration of the soul is measured not in kilometers, but in fathoms, and each of us has a place hidden within us where we are invited to dive deep, so that the knowing (and unknowing) encoded within us may surface in our lives.

This is what brings us to the "journey to the wild heart," the lovely and powerful metaphor that guides Amy Frykholm—and now us—as we join her on this interior passage. She distills the insights and intuitions from her own travels (inner and outer) into one of the most succinct and accessible frameworks for reflection and contemplation that I have ever come across.

Like the four movements of a symphony or the four seasons of a year, she offers us a simple and infinitely scalable four-step process by which we can respond to any moment, or place, or feeling, or perception, taking it deeper and getting to know it from every angle. And she gives us a wealth of exercises to put this process into motion. But the real gift here consists of how easily this framework for inward discovery can leap off the pages of the book and into your ongoing contemplative toolbox.

By the time you finish this book, you will have discovered a new template for spiritual reflection that you can use in any context, any time you find life offering you another chance to take that deep inner dive. This fourfold invitation is steeped in the great tradition of mystical spirituality, while at the same time it's fresh and new.

This is a marvelous book to bring with you on a retreat, or a pilgrimage like the Camino, or maybe just a solitary week listening to the surf on your favorite beach. But it's not just an optional resource for those exterior journeys—after all, the wondrous heart is a haven of wilderness wherever it beats—so bring these four invitations into your sitting room or your neighborhood coffee shop.

Ignatius of Loyola is famous for inviting those he counseled to seek God in all things, and Julian of Norwich declared that "the fullness of joy is to behold God in all" (I love how open-ended Julian's words are: does she mean to remind us that we can meet God in all things? All people? All circumstances? Julian, like the Spirit, leaves all possibilities open). If words like these land like a melody in your soul, then the experience that awaits you in the pages to come will seem like an old friend, and lingering over them will be a grace-filled gift. And if the idea of seeking (or finding) God in the everyday warp and weft of your life leaves you feeling puzzled or bemused, then please, by all means, read this book—and embrace the practices with an open mind and a sense of leisure, for the wisdom in this book is not to be rushed. It's a gentle path but it can take you to some very deep places indeed.

I believe that introductions to books are like sermons or arguments with your spouse—the shorter they are, the better. So I will sign off now, and leave you to turn the page and embark upon your adventure.

Follow the highway to your wild heart: enjoy the songs and the music of nature, but remember to listen for the silence as well.

Introduction

Into the Journey

This book is an invitation to a journey on the rocky trail to contemplative living. If you've picked this book up, you're likely in search of a richer, fuller, deeper spiritual life, and you know that within you there is a wild heart that yearns for this life. Every pilgrimage—whether it is an interior soul-searching, a stay-in-place retreat, or a pilgrimage to near and far places—sends us on a treasure hunt through our own souls. This book is meant as a guide for that hunt.

Once upon a time, as this kind of story often begins, I set out on a journey in search of the wild heart. My particular search took two forms: one was looking for a deeper life, and the other was looking for the trail of a historical woman whose life embodied that search for me. Her name was Mary of Egypt. She was a fifth-century saint who, after living as a runaway, a prostitute, and a spiritual seeker, took up residence in the wilderness of Jordan, where she lived as a hermit. A great deal of the practices, equipment, and tools I offer in this book come from my search for her. But they are also woven into my daily life, teaching, observing, practicing, and paying attention to how other people pursue contemplative living. The search is everywhere, around us all the time. And so are the treasures. I can say with full confidence that if you seek, you will find.

It has been my experience that as we take these journeys, the wild, contemplative heart emerges, not from new forms of knowledge or a quick ten-step guide, but from the integration and expansion of what we *don't* know, what contemplatives call the *via avia*, the way of no way. Even though others have gone before us, the way isn't prescribed but often made as we go along and as we let go of old certainties and expectations.

All of us will come into these invitations differently and move through the landscape at our own pace, seeking and finding through an inner guidance that no writer of any book can predict. I found, as I followed Mary of Egypt through her own landscape, that she got wilder as I went, and that she opened up spaces inside me that were unpredictable. She wilded me. I detail this in my book *Wild Woman: A Footnote, the Desert, and My Quest for an Elusive Saint.*

In the icons of her that exist, she appears as an archetypal wild woman, often with unkempt hair, mostly naked, in a barren landscape. Sometimes she holds a skull in her hands. Other times, she lifts her hands in prayer. She appears like an iconic female pair to John the Baptist, both of them children of the wilderness.

And as you travel on this journey, your own guides will lead you toward your own wild heart. All of us have people who appear in our lives and characterize aspects of our own selves that we long to bring into being. We feel this longing, and we also feel the fear of breaking the boundaries as we attempt to live braver and fuller lives.

The story of Mary of Egypt details just one way that the wild heart can unfold inside each of us, and the relentless love that God has for us. Mary began her journey as a runaway child, leaving the part of Egypt that she had called home, and going to the city of Alexandria. There, she survived by any means necessary: begging, spinning flax, and prostitution. One day, she saw pilgrims headed to the Feast of the Holy Cross in Jerusalem. Her curiosity stirred, she found a way to join their boat sailing the Mediterranean Sea by selling sex to her fellow travelers. Arriving on the shore of what is now Israel, she continued to follow the pilgrims as they made their way to the Church of the Holy Sepulchre, in Jerusalem.

Once there, even as other pilgrims flowed through the doors, she found she could not enter the church. Some mysterious force kept her back. Left behind in the court-yard, she encountered an icon of the Virgin Mary. She began to talk to the icon, and a dialogue of sorts took shape that led her to discern and articulate her deepest desire: to begin a new life.

After she discovered this desire, she was able to enter the church. But after she venerated the Holy Cross, she had no idea what to do next. She heard a voice that said, "Cross the river and you will find a beautiful rest." She found her way from Jerusalem to the Jordan River. Cross-ing its banks, she entered the wilderness of what is now Jordan, where she lived for the rest of her life as a desert hermit, being taught, she says, by the Virgin Mary herself.

While this account of Mary's life was written down in the seventh century, it contained so much piety and the imagined saintliness of another time that I found it dif-ficult to find Mary's story within the story. As I traveled in search of her, I found myself asking, "What is at the heart of what Mary discovered in the desert? Could I also find it?" I wasn't the only one asking this question. The monk who found her in the wilderness, Zosimas, became her student and called her "she who would not be held." He also spent his later life trying to learn about the wild heart of contemplation from her.

Gradually I found—and am still finding—that inner story of the wild heart. As I walked the path that Mary took in her life, I found that the wild call of the Tristan's starling, the oleander cascading over rocks, the darting dragonflies and their abandoned larval shells began to open up the space inside me that had felt formal and closed, built on the niceties of another time. Mary's story—the story of a runaway, a prostitute, a woman on the run, a desert solitary—resonated deep inside. She was calling me toward what folklorist Clarissa Pinkola Estés calls "a deeper life, a full life, a sane life."

Out of this experience come the four invitations that shape this book. This book is written on the premise that entering the wild heart of contemplative living can be as simple (and as challenging) as developing a particular form of attention, wherever you are. Anthropologists Edith and Victor Turner who wrote about religion and liminality describe pilgrimage as "extroverted mysticism" and mysticism as "introverted pilgrimage." Both involve an acute attention to one's inner life and one's particular circumstances. So with this intention we will travel together: to go inward and to move outward, listening, observing, and allowing the mysterious work of the Spirit.

Before I detail the invitations themselves, I want to point out that these invitations can be practiced by yourself or in community. I've attempted to describe some ways that you might use this book in both settings. But if you are conducting these various experiments by yourself, your efforts are not isolated. The monks of the Christian desert believed that all the work they did in solitude had direct bearing on the wider world. They entered into the desert *for* the world, not from the world.

In her book *How to Do Nothing*, contemporary, secular contemplative Jenny Odell writes that "if there are sanctuaries, they are less places to bury your head in the sand, than places where different languages of time and being are kept alive." I hope that you might find these places—where other forms of time and being are kept alive—in the journeys you take through these invitations. Such sanctuaries are intimately connected to contemplative living, an essential part of its nature. We seek them out, not because we are attempting to hide from the contemporary world, but because we are seeking to fully engage the world at a deeper level of its existence and our own.

And at the same time, even if you undertake these journeys with companions, you also travel alone. The spiritual journey is highly individualized, even as it is intensely communal. You must find your own way, tune in to your own inner voice. No one can do this for you. The spiritual journey, says contemplative monastic Thomas Keating, is a "very slow and plodding journey to the truth that involves the dismantling of all the nonsense." As we travel toward the wild heart, we let go of the various forms of nonsense that have held us—social and personal, familial and cultural. And we release forms of certainty that no longer have value for the way forward. We find truth in the slant and circuitous path that we might never have guessed was ours to travel.

So while the sequence I have laid out in these four invitations—discover, behold, bewilder, and discern—is intentional, the path is never linear.

The first two invitations—discover and behold—involve forms of knowing. The invitation to discover trains us to follow patterns within ourselves, the looping, winding golden thread that William Blake promises leads us to the Holy City, to "Jerusalem's wall," a place of the wild heart. The invitation to behold teaches us to set aside our previous certainties and closely observe, as best we can, something outside ourselves. This may be a natural phenomenon, a text, another human being, or even sometimes, a stranger inside ourselves.

But then, we embark further, working through uncertainty, toward an invitation to bewilderment. We allow our knowing to take us into unknowing. This process can be uncomfortable and challenging, but it is essential to our transformation. One of the first things Jesus says to the crowd in the Gospel of Mark is *Metanoeite!* which can be literally translated "Go beyond your mind." Bewilderment is an essential step in the contemplative journey because we practice undoing ourselves so that we can expand into the widening experience of grace.

And finally we take up the invitation to discern. I've often wanted discernment to be an experience of absolute clarity (and at least once, it was!), but I've found in the journey to the wild heart that discernment might be better understood as a form of play. We try to play out the results of our explorations, wonder about them, respond to their shy signals with an attempt to find words. These are often tiny answers, hidden help, that are more akin to the light of a firefly than to a spotlight. Discernment appears, lights up the dark for a moment, and then the darkness comes back in again. So for the purposes of this book, we will take the firefly approach to discernment: accepting the darkness, appreciating it, and then loving and offering gratitude to the small flashes of light as they appear.

In Part I, I lay out each of the invitations in detail. In Part II, I play out cycles of exercises that engage the invitations. I call each cycle a session. The word *session* comes from Robert Farrar Capon's book *The Supper of the Lamb*, as he invites his readers to gather for a "Session, a meeting, a society of things." A session is an incarnational experience where the world as it is comes together with the particularities of your own attention and the presence of God. In the midst of the sessions, the four invitations become interlocking puzzle pieces, each relying on the other and creatively building on the other.

This book is meant to be flexible in its use—for multiple applications, various life situations and times. You might use it for your own personal exploration during daily times that you set aside. For example, during a period of transition, you might set aside an hour a day to work through this book and its exercises, allowing the work to mingle with daily life and its demands. You can work at your own pace and trust that guidance will emerge as you do so.

You might also take this book along on a retreat or on a pilgrimage and use the exercises in those settings to be more fully awake to your surroundings and to the hidden help available to you in those places. These exercises are nothing if not portable, like a backpack of spiritual support that you can take with you on those inner and outer journeys that can feel perilous.

Finally, you might try using this book in a study group, on a group retreat, or over time with a companion. Each meeting can be a "session," where together you explore what is available to you and share what you learn along the way. In these settings, it's vital that the spiritual journey of each is respected and attended without anyone in the group determined to find a certain outcome. There are no certain outcomes—except, I hope, that you will know yourself and your own spiritual path more deeply.

Although each session is intended to work together as an interconnected unit of exercises, the invitations in each session are not equal in length. Some invitations are a simple ten minutes, but others might require you to set aside a larger block of time in order to allow yourself to go deep. You might want to read through an entire session and plan out the time that will work for you. The sessions list basic materials that you likely have nearby: a favorite book, a timer, colored pencils, a journal, and so forth, that help you explore an invitation. And timer settings are suggestions as a starting point, but there's no need to hurry through any particular session or exercise. I've found that the first impulse that comes to mind in response to an exercise prompt is just as good as any other impulse. And you can take one exercise per day instead of an entire session at once. One session might also be adapted for an entire retreat day, with breaks in between. Or you may find that you need more time because of what is stirring in you. This too is unpredictable.

The sessions, the exercises, the recommendations—everything that follows here—rely on your consent. There's no bullying on a spiritual path. This is consent to your own goodness, first and foremost, consent to your gifts, consent to letting go, and consent to the workings of the Spirit within you. You are a living, breathing manifestation of the mystical tradition: you, right now, whatever you are doing or thinking at this moment. As you find it within yourself to undertake this journey, you will be met by a wild, openhearted, infinitely generous God. Pay attention to your own wild heart and to all that is around you, and you will find your next brave step.

invitations

Invitation One

Discover

The invitation to discover begins with the golden thread I mentioned in the introduction in a poem by William Blake:

> I give you the end of a golden string;
> Only wind it into a ball,
> It will lead you in at Heaven's gate,
> Built in Jerusalem's wall.

This is a thread that runs through your life, through all of our lives, but it is often difficult to find and to follow. In this invitation, we look for and follow this thread by engaging in a writing practice. The American contemplative poet William Stafford noted that the golden thread is most often found in the details of our lives, and he believed, as the poet Robert Bly put it, that "every detail—the sound of the lawn mower, the memory of your father's hands, a crack you once heard in lake ice, the jogger hurtling herself past your window—will lead you to amazing riches."

Once Bly asked if Stafford really believed that every detail was a thread or if he meant that there were particular details that became the golden thread. "No," Stafford replied emphatically. "Every thread. . . . My faith is that any old thread will do."[1]

The thread mysteriously begins inside you and leads you to whatever is most holy in yourself. Jerusalem's wall is that place where the spiritual journey takes us. For the purposes of our work here, it is synonymous with the wild heart: the place inside us that is most attuned to God's working, most interested in our transformation, and most alive.

We begin with the details of our lives: the smell and feel of the air in the room where we are right now, the light, the voices of the people in the next room. All of these are the ends of the golden thread, and our work, in the invitation to discover, is to find the thread and to follow it.

So, take any pen and any paper—a notebook, your

---

[1] Conversation between Bly and Stafford: https://www.williamstafford. org/the-golden-thread.

journal, the back of an envelope. It can be elevated—like a handmade, leather-bound journal—to remind you that this is a sacred process. Or it can be scratch paper—to remind you not to take yourself too seriously. Already you are following your instincts, listening to what works best for you.

Then simply sit down anywhere: at a table, in a chair, at your desk, under a tree, at the airport, on a bus. Set a timer and begin with a prompt. It might be a line from a poem, a ray of light that is falling on the table in front of you, or even Blake's golden thread. Following the prompt, write anything and everything that comes to your head, not trying to predetermine the outcome, not already knowing what you will say. Feel the anxiety, the excitement, perhaps even the fear of the start of a journey.

Stafford gives a little bit more instruction that I think is essential for this invitation. In his essay, "The End of a Golden String," he writes, "The stance to take, reading or writing, is neutral, ready, susceptible to now."

Neutral, ready, susceptible to now. The Spirit's work within us is always in the now, and it is always more than we can expect or imagine. So we orient ourselves to the present moment with this open stance. Prepared, yes, like anyone embarking on a journey, but also ready to be led anywhere.

But what appears on the surface as the simplest of all practices also reveals complexities. One problem, as you may already know by the pain in your chest that just came up when I mentioned writing, is that most people think that writing is an opportunity for judgment. The act of putting pen to paper reminds us of the red marks that a teacher put on our papers in school or of a parent who rewrote everything that we turned in because what we'd done wasn't good enough or a college professor whose criticisms are still ringing in our ears decades later. Writing, even if we long to do it, reminds us of anything and everything except a simple and elemental form of following the golden thread.

But this is exactly why writing is the essential practice in the invitation to discover. Everyone who is reading this book learned to write at some time or another, by which I mean learned the basic practice of putting a pen to paper and moving it across the page. You don't need any special expertise. You don't need nice handwriting or good spelling. The Spirit guiding your hand couldn't care less and won't give you a gold star for penmanship.

For each discovery exercise, you will be given a new prompt and a time limit, with the goal being to simply write until the timer goes off. A few tricks can be handy in allowing the golden thread to lead you, instead of your ego or your inner critic. If you find that you can't think of anything to write on the paper, simply write the prompt over and over until the stuttering in your brain gives way.

I highly recommend, following writing teacher Natalie

Goldberg, that you do not cross out or edit as you write. When we cross out, we signal to the inner golden thread follower that what we're really doing here is judging. The follower gets confused, because following the golden thread and editing are two very different brain functions. They have to be done separately. Discovery is done without reference to quality. As Stafford says, "Any little impulse is accepted and enhanced."

So we keep going, even when a voice in our head tells us that what we're doing is no good, of little use, would be embarrassing for someone else to find, and so on. In Jewish tradition, this voice is called the *yetzer harah*, the inner adversary, and while it has its purposes, it has little use while you are embarking on this journey of discovery.

I also recommend you do your discovery exercises with pen and paper and not on a computer. This is because we all first learned to write by holding a writing instrument in our hands, and the child inside of us has a much better idea how to follow the golden thread than the later adult who learned to use a computer. When we take up a pen and put it on the paper, we are engaging in a deeper and more fundamental relationship with our inner listening than computers can allow us. Also most of us use computers to connect to the outside world. We send messages through them; they are means to our public personas; they often signal "work"; and it is very difficult to get a sufficient sense of privacy and deep listening through them.

So when you begin these exercises, set aside your distractions and search for the elemental part of yourself that intuits how to follow the golden thread using pen and paper. Even if you are a little rusty with your handwriting, that rustiness is your friend. It will allow you to be available to something new.

Many of us were taught to think that we were good or bad at writing. At the very least, we were convinced that other people were better, and so every act of writing, however private, has become an act of comparison. We were shamed by our grammar and spelling mistakes or our own syntactical peculiarities. We were told that our writing didn't measure up to a standard invented by someone else or, even worse for following the golden thread, we got an A+. Furthermore, we became terrified of self-exposure on the page and so we invented a thousand ways to avoid our own sincerity.

It does take time and practice to use this method for discovery. Even after years of using this method to understand myself, my spiritual life, and my creative work better, I still find myself asking, "How sincere are you being?" I still look for a way to follow the golden thread "without wax"—the literal meaning of the word *sincere*. This is a practice that seems to strip away, a little at a time, the vanities and self-certainties that I carry to the page and reveal to me the golden thread that I am always, already following.

Recently, I've been gathering people around my dining room table to practice discovery together. They come from all walks of life with all kinds of intentions related to their writing. Perhaps what has most surprised me in the gatherings is the amount of resistance that all of us bring to a simple writing practice, and then the surprising amount of corresponding joy that comes as we've worked through our resistance and found the golden thread in unexpected places.

For example, one time we began with the simple prompt, "I remember . . ." I set the timer for ten minutes and people began to write. Some filled the page with only one memory—teasing out every detail they could. Some repeated, "I remember, I remember, I remember . . ." getting everything from the memory of Twinkies at the corner store to their grandfather's preference for tomato and onion sandwiches onto the page in their first ten minutes. For each person the golden thread took a different form, and practitioners gradually discovered what was most alive inside them by feeling how it took shape on the page.

What I continue to learn from this discovery practice is that it doesn't matter where we start. The golden thread always appears and shapes the path. We could start with a tube of toothpaste at the center of the table or "What is the most important thing that ever happened to you?"—both lead to unexpected places that do not seem to be directed by us. This practice claims a world imbued with God's presence. It is invested, fundamentally, in a sacramental worldview: that the details of our lives matter. That God is at work in us and through us—not in an abstract sense, but in one that unfolds at the level of daily life. But we have to return again and again to our contemplative stance: neutral, ready, susceptible to now.

This stance is essential. Even while the details of our lives matter, paradoxically, we are also going to be gradually undone. Our preconceived ideas will be worn away. We will be trained in the Spirit's own perception of the now of our lives. We do this because we signal to our inner lives that we are not in control of the process, that we are open to the guidance of the Holy Spirit, and that we will listen as best as we can. As eighteenth-century Jesuit Jean-Pierre de Caussade writes in his book *Abandonment to Divine Providence*, "The present moment is always full of infinite treasure; it contains far more than you have the capacity to hold. Faith is the measure: what you find in the present moment will be according to your faith. Love is the measure: the more your heart loves, the more it desires, and the more it desires, the more it finds."

In my own attempts to follow the golden thread in the life of Mary of Egypt, I went detail to detail through my days. Even with the difficulties of travel logistics, the heat, and the fact that when you are on the road, you can't control what is happening around and to you,

I tried to taste the coffee I was sipping, learn the name of the tree I was sitting under, and connect with the people who had presented themselves as my guides for that day and that moment. Then every night, I returned to my room and took stock, through writing, of what I had seen and heard. I could not immediately make sense of much of it, and often a day's disparate events seemed devoid of meaning, too fragmented for the process of golden-thread finding. But gradually, through an openhearted process of discovery, I could begin to see how meaning was unfolding, how I was a part of a collaborative process with the Spirit, how to take hold of the golden thread gently and not pull too hard.

This is the best way I know to open ourselves to the riches of the journey, available everywhere, including within ourselves.

Discover: Companions and Guides

Bly, Robert. Introduction to *The Darkness Around Us Is Deep: Selected Poems of William Stafford.* San Francisco: HarperPerennial, 1993.

Brown, Valerie. *Hope Leans Forward: Braving Your Way toward Simplicity, Awakening, and Peace.* Minneapolis: Broadleaf, 2022.

Cameron, Julia. *The Artist's Way: A Spiritual Path to Higher Creativity.* New York: Putnam, 1992.

de Caussade, Jean-Pierre. *Abandonment to Divine Providence.* Translated by E. J. Strickland. San Francisco: Ignatius Press, 2011.

Estés, Clarissa Pinkola. *Women Who Run with the Wolves: Myths and Stories of the Wild Woman Archetype.* New York: Ballantine Books, 1995.

Gbowee, Leymah, with Carol Mithers. *Mighty Be Our Powers: How Sisterhood, Prayer, and Sex Changed a Nation at War.* New York: Beast Books, 2011.

Goldberg, Natalie. *Writing Down the Bones.* Boston: Shambhala, 1986.

Kimmerer, Robin. *Braiding Sweetgrass.* Minneapolis: Milkweed, 2013.

Shapiro, Rami, and Aaron Shapiro. *Writing—The Sacred Art: Beyond the Page to Spiritual Practice.* Woodstock, VT: Skylight Paths, 2012.

Shepherd, Philip. *New Self, New World: Recovering Our Senses in the Twenty-First Century.* Berkeley, CA: North Atlantic Books, 2010.

Stafford, William. "The End of a Golden String." In *Writing the Australian Crawl: Views on the Writer's Vocation.* Ann Arbor: University of Michigan Press, 1978.

Wahlstrom, Ralph L. *The Tao of Writing: Imagine. Create. Flow.* Avon, MA: Adams Media, 2006.

Invitation Two

Behold

In *The Supper of the Lamb: A Culinary Reflection*, Episco-pal priest Robert Farrar Capon spends the entire book reflecting on one recipe, a recipe for lamb stew. He takes readers through every aspect of preparation—physical and spiritual—as if this stew were the most sacred dish ever made. In one chapter, which he calls, "The First Ses-sion," he encourages readers to take an hour to chop an onion. You sit with the onion. You carefully observe it. You allow yourself to be in its company. You slowly, in admiration and affection, chop it. "Admittedly," Capon writes, "spending an hour in the society of an onion may be something you have never done before."

It's a shocking and even humorous suggestion: to spend an hour with an onion. But Capon is referring to a spiritual practice that is essential to the journey toward the wild heart: beholding. Beholding is the practice of being in the presence of something or someone and contemplating it, allowing your own reality to be penetrated by the reality of this other. Like the discovery practice, describing beholding is deceptively simple. You sit in front of an object, a person, a situation, and contemplate it without attempting to change it for as long as you've set a timer for. As your attention wanders, you gently return your attention to the object of your contemplation in an act of loving attention.

Inspired by Capon's contemplative meditation and his beholding of the onion, I once asked a group of students in a workshop to "behold" an orange. Each student was given a navel orange that I had purchased at the local grocery store. Now, I said, take it anywhere you want so you can truly spend time and behold the orange. We were on a college campus in summer, so there were empty classrooms and lots of outside space; there were tables at the library and benches under big trees.

My idea of moving out of the classroom and into the larger world had to do with my sense that it would be difficult to transition to a space in which you could be in a meaningful engagement with an orange, holding a long gaze. I thought students might need some privacy. There is something almost embarrassing about the rawness of a contemplative gaze, a relational engagement, the way it jolts things inside us, surprises us, and moves us. It's remarkably vulnerable and strange to the ego.

The truth is, when I gave this assignment, I'd never done it myself. I'd spent a lot of time debating what object to choose, and I'd thought about bringing knives and cutting boards and onions. In the end, I'd chosen an orange because it wasn't as smelly as an onion. And I wouldn't need those knives and cutting boards. Oranges are easy to transport, and they were abundantly available at the local grocery store. They are quite a convenient little package.

But also, Capon says, if you are hoping to "look the world back into grace," then peel an orange.

> Do it lovingly—in perfect quarters like little boats, or in staggered exfoliations like a flat map of the round world, or in one long spiral as my grandfather used to do. Nothing is more likely to become garbage than orange rind, but for as long as anyone looks at it in delight, it stands a million triumphant miles from the trash heap.

I was hoping that students would grasp what Capon so beautifully expresses, but I had no idea what would come of time spent beholding an orange. I was nervous about it. It seemed the height of folly to assign students something you had never done yourself.

But as these four invitations weave in and around

each other, Behold brought me back around again to Discover: Why had I never done it? How much would it have cost me to sit with an orange for even fifteen minutes in preparation for class? Nothing. And I still didn't do it. Philosopher Simone Weil describes this resistance perfectly. "Something in our soul has a far more violent repugnance for true attention than the flesh has for bodily fatigue." Beholding requires overcoming that repugnance, that resistance, that excuse-making part of ourselves. And it is hard work. But it's work built in relation: I personally needed, and continue to need, the company and encouragement of others to practice it.

Even though a lot of my usual instincts worked against this, I gave the students a full hour for this exercise. There's no rushing it. I knew they would feel restless, unproductive, and foolish as they sat there hanging out with an orange. It would feel like jumping into a cold pool. There would be resistance. Moving from the unrealness of our ordinary consciousness toward the reality of an encounter is a move full of mysterious fear.

What in the world is there to be afraid of? It's just an orange. It's just time. And yet we are afraid, and the reason is simple: to enter into relation, a part of us that is very fierce and very in control and very sure of everything has to step aside and soften. This encounter involves a tiny act of kenosis—self-surrendering love—and the ego isn't inclined in this way.

But there is also a saving grace. There is always a saving grace. Our senses. "If you can't see what you are looking for," says Mark Nepo in his book *The Exquisite Risk*, "see what's there. It's enough." That's never a bad place to start a session. At the time when I gave this assignment, I thought only of our five senses, and I still think they are wonderfully accessible. But since then I've come to name other things that are sensory as well. For example, we have an innate sense of space—the space around us and the space within us. We have an inner sense of balance. We can perceive the passage of time—duration. We can perceive location—an inner perception of where something is. Synesthesia is the means by which some people can hear colors or see sounds. The realm of perception is much richer than our five senses alone.

But to begin, the orange is rich in sensory detail of the basic five senses type. The smell of the orange, if taken in deeply, can change from moment to moment revealing not only its own nuances, but also emotional responses within the smeller. The feel of an orange is remarkable, and most of us have never really spent any time with its peel or the soft interior or the pith, or with the oil that sprays out and gets onto your fingers. Try staring at the navel of an orange for five minutes and see what happens inside of you. And then there's the fact that on top of all of that, an orange is unbelievably sweet and tart and dances on the tongue. Its gifts go on and on.

The results of the classroom experiment were astonishing. Students returned to class both in tears and in silence. "I just had a spiritual experience," one student said quietly, *"with an orange!"* I too was moved, tears forming in my eyes at the vulnerability of the orange, the way that it offers itself to the world so openly. During the time of the experiment, its skin became my skin. Its unveiling was my unveiling. Its sweetness became an unexpected and undeserved gift. These things are hard to put into words unless you've met with, been in relation to, an orange. It sounds insane, but the experience itself takes you into the heart of things in a way that is transformative. It led me to believe that this experience, this astonishment, is available to us all the time, everywhere.

Let's be clear, though, contemplation of any object, person, idea, or being is much more difficult than it sounds. First of all, we face the difficulty of sitting down for beholding at all. There is always one more thing to do that is more important than spending time with an orange. Maybe the problem lies in the very metaphor of "spending" time. When we think we are spending our precious time on nothing, wasting it (another metaphor), the value of a relationship is invisible to us. Being productive, useful, turning our own selves into objects for others to use feels much more appropriate than settling in to see what might or might not emerge in this humble meeting.

Don't underestimate the paradigm shift required for the

act of beholding, just how different it is from our everyday lives and just how shiny and compelling our everyday life will seem when we propose pausing for some time beholding. In our society, we talk frequently about the pull of technology, and no doubt, technology is bent on destroying what threads of attention we still possess. But the problem we are describing is much older in human nature than our cell phones.

If we are able to get ourselves situated for beholding, we will notice the next difficulty arising: We are constantly being taken out of presence into our own thoughts. While contemplating the orange, I had to return to the orange again and again, disappearing for whole minutes into my thought world, into my anxiety. Was I doing this right? What kind of experience were the students having? What was the cafeteria going to serve for lunch? Why do Lutherans sing all six verses of every hymn? This kind of wandering in attention is completely normal and doesn't mean I was doing the exercise wrong.

Any act of attention is not a sustained experiencing. It's a series of successive efforts to bring attention back to the same thing, considering it again and again. This kind of encounter is a series of repeated acts of will. We gradually train our attention to encounter, discovering its fruits in slow and subtle movements over time. Whatever you behold, you eventually become beholden to. You enter into a love relation. You recognize your own dependence on the created world, the way that you are held, even as you are holding.

And sometimes grace carries us away, and we glimpse, maybe even for several seconds at a time, the whole interconnected, openhearted world that welcomes an orange and welcomes us. "If you want to become full," the ancient wisdom text *Tao te Ching* advises, "let yourself become empty." As we practice the self-emptying process of beholding, we can notice the ways that attention softens and opens us, introduces the possibility of deeply rooted joy, and then allows us to carry that joy to others.

The benefits of this practice are enormous—not just for us personally, but for all that we are connected to (which, of course, is everything). "To be naked, to be poor, to have nothing, to be empty transforms nature; emptiness makes water flow uphill, and many other marvels of which we need not now speak," Meister Eckhart writes in *The Book of Divine Consolation*, mysteriously hinting at what might be hiding in the simple practice of learning to empty ourselves and train our attention.

Like the invitation to discover, this practice became an essential part of my life when I was in search of Mary of Egypt. How could I differentiate my experience from the glancing, selfie-taking forms of attention that were so much a part of what I knew of travel? Every day, I decided, wherever I was and whatever I was up to, I would attempt to sit and behold. I would choose a spot that was the closest I could come to Mary of Egypt on that particular day, and then I would train my attention in loving acceptance of whatever was there. This was a discipline more than a "discovery" practice. I simply tried to place my own assumptions, busyness, and agenda under the circumstances that I found myself in. In this way, I tried to allow other ways of knowing and being in the world to encounter me.

Hiding behind the humble encounter with any earthly being is what Jewish philosopher Martin Buber calls an "intimation of the eternal Thou." "What is greater for us," he writes, "than enigmatic webs at the margins of being is the central actuality of an everyday hour on earth, with a streak of sunshine on a maple twig and an intimation of the eternal Thou" (Martin Buber, *I and Thou*). The practice of beholding allows us to put into practice what Simone Weil calls the "foundation of the spiritual life": waiting in expectation. If we are patient, gentle, and careful, the world will unfold in front of us, revealing its hidden wholeness.

Behold: Companions and Guides

Buber, Martin. *I and Thou.* Translated by Ronald Gregor Smith. New York: Simon and Schuster, 2023.

Butcher, Carmen Acevedo. *Practice of the Presence: A Revolutionary Translation of the Writings of Brother*

Lawrence of the Resurrection. Minneapolis: Broadleaf Books, 2022.

Capon, Robert Farrar. *Supper of the Lamb: A Culinary Reflection.* New York: Harcourt Brace Jovanovich, 1969.

Curtice, Kaitlin. *Living Resistance: An Indigenous Vision for Seeking Wholeness Every Day.* Grand Rapids, MI: Brazos Press, 2023.

Eckhart, Meister. *The Book of Divine Consolation*, excerpted in *Selections from His Essential Writings.* Translation by Edmund College. Edited by Emilie Griffin. San Francisco: HarperSanFrancisco, 1981.

Keating, Thomas. *Intimacy with God: An Introduction to Centering Prayer.* New York: Crossroad, 2019.

Laird, Martin. *Into the Silent Land: A Guide to the Christian Practice of Contemplation.* New York: Oxford University Press, 2006.

Odell, Jenny. *How to Do Nothing: Resisting the Attention Economy.* Brooklyn, NY: Melville House, 2019.

Paintner, Christine Valters. *The Soul of a Pilgrim: Eight Practices for the Journey Within.* Notre Dame, IN: Sorin Books, 2015.

Thurman, Howard. *For the Inward Journey.* New York: Harcourt Brace Jovanovich, 1984.

Weil, Simone. "Reflections on the Right Use of School Studies with a View to the Love of God." In *The Simone Weil Reader*, edited by George A. Panichas. Mt. Kisco, NY: Moyer Bell, 1977.

Invitation Three

Bewilder

Both of the invitations to discover and behold engage two distinct ways of knowing. As we practice free writing, we use the familiar means of pen and paper to know our own minds, experiences, and situations better. As we sit in a posture of beholding, we allow the world outside ourselves to penetrate our experience, and so we know it a bit better.

But the third invitation—bewildering—is different. It is a practice of unknowing, and it is considerably more difficult both to describe and to enact. And yet it is essential on the journey to the wild heart. When Mary of Egypt arrived at the Jordan River on her journey to the wild heart, it wasn't enough that she had discovered God's own grace threaded through her life, and it wasn't even enough that she had encountered Mary through the icon at the Church of the Holy Sepulchre. The work she had to do now, and it was a work she describes lasting seventeen years, was to undo herself, to enter into a process of unknowing, where her assumptions about the world had to be unmade in order for her to find healing. She had, in other words, to become bewildered, and this was the part of Mary's journey that most beckoned to me when I started my own.

For me, Mary's journey is deeply rooted in the call in the gospels of *metanoia*. In the Gospel of Mark, as I noted earlier, one of the first things Jesus says to the crowd gathered at the Jordan is *Metanoeite!* What does this strange word mean? Traditionally, there is no mystery. The word has been fairly consistently translated as "repent!" for all of its history in the English language.

There are good theological reasons for translating this word in this way, but the two words come from very different roots. *Metanoeite* comes from two Greek roots. *Meta* means "beyond." We can still use this root this way in English. Metaphysics, for example, means beyond the physical. Meta is the name that Mark Zuckerberg chose for his company, perhaps because it suggested something that goes beyond the ordinary circumstances of daily life. *Noia* comes from the Greek word *nous*. *Nous* is a complex concept in biblical Greek. It is usually translated as "mind," although this is because our understandings of the self in contemporary English are somewhat more limited than Greek conceptions of the self. But without going too much into the weeds, let's just say, *nous* is a form of the self that knows, that is engaged in knowing. So *metanoiete* could be more precisely translated as "go beyond what you know" or "go beyond your mind."

Repent comes from two Latin roots. *Re* is an intensification and *pent* is the feeling of having done something wrong. So repent is, at its roots, a bad feeling about oneself—"very much to regret" is an exact translation. You can see how different these two words are conceptually, and why the Greek suggests transformation in a way that the Latin-derived English does not.

One of Jesus's most central commands is not to a feeling, but to a form of unknowing. When Mary of Egypt began her tutelage in the desert, this is precisely the path that she was on. She had concepts of the world and of herself that could not be carried forward in her new life. She asked Mary, the Mother of God, whom she embraced as her teacher in the courtyard of the church, to remake her. As her story is told, those seventeen years were arduous ones to bind up and heal old wounds, and then to come into a presence and an awareness of herself in relation to both God and to the wild world around her. As ingrained as our habits of self are, it's hard to believe that our inner life can be renewed. Renewal takes patience and courage, commitment and fortitude—and bewilderment.

We too are asked to go beyond our preconceived notions of the world, our assumptions, our certainties, and allow ourselves to enter a state of bewilderment.

Our minds and ourselves are habits. Much contemporary neuroscience has gone into helping us understand this. Neuroscientists have demonstrated what they've called the "default mode network" in the brain: ways the brain sets up perception and understanding. The default mode network is believed to be involved in everything from memory to self-understanding to empathy to social judgments to setting goals—the list goes on and on. In other words, we are set up to think the same thoughts in the same way over and over again, to confirm our experience in the world through a kind of imperceptible inner training. But, Jesus says, that is not all that we are or can be.

In Buddhism, there is also a teaching about this, another way of looking at the need for *metanoia*: that our self's seeming solidity and stability is an illusion. In Norman Fischer's book *Training in Compassion*, the Buddhist teacher talks about how we learn to perceive ourselves in certain ways to the exclusion of other ways. "The sense we have of ourselves," he argues, "is not what our self actually feels like. This is an astonishing thing to contemplate: that the person we feel inside is a distortion of some kind, a bad habit." Fischer argues that there is another self amid that distortion, a self he calls "the principal witness" of our lives. Most of us never meet that other self because we are completely caught up in the ways of being and knowing created by our default mode networks.

So how do we get beyond these default perceptions of ourselves? Is there a practice for this? The truth is that we are, as human beings, always in the midst of transformation. The world is always more bewildering and more openhearted and more generous than we can perceive, and we are always being changed and shaped by it. And furthermore, God is always already at work in our lives, always already helping us to see the next steps and to take them, even if we have to act against our self-certainties.

But bewilderment, or as I began to hear it in my study of Mary of Egypt—Be Wilder Ment—can be cultivated. Many of us in Christian contemplative tradition began a cultivation of bewilderment through the practice of centering prayer, when for a few moments each day, we pause and remember that we are not in control of our lives. In the silence and in what Julian of Norwich calls the Spirit's "sweet touching," we are gradually transformed, allowed to release the old casings that have held us trapped, and enter into the new life that God is preparing for us.

Our best guides in the process of bewilderment are often artists, who place themselves routinely in front of ordinary things and try to see them anew. I think of Cézanne in front of his pears, as he tries to see the life and color and beauty in them and tries to show you how to see that too. I think of a French writer named Georges Perec who sat in one corner of Paris for three days straight trying to record everything he saw about everyday life: it was both an act of beholding and bewildering simultaneously, as many bewildering practices are. It takes time to unsee what we always see, to unknow what we are so sure of.

When I was in search of Mary of Egypt, bewilderment became a part of my everyday life because I was in search of something that I didn't already know. By the time I reached the Monastery of St. Gerasimos near Jericho, I was exhausted by my own search. I was ready to throw in the towel on the whole adventure and confess that it had been a great big exercise in failure. I sat in the pews in the little church there with a nun in Birkenstocks sleeping on a bench outside, and I cried.

The next day, emptied by my sense of failure, I crossed the border between Israel and Jordan and put my fate in the hands of a guide named Jawad, a secular Muslim accountant and wilderness expert. He was about as far from my idea of a person who could lead me to Mary of Egypt as I could imagine. But anyway, I'd given up on that. I was baffled that I had come this far, tried this hard, and had nothing to show for it.

Within an hour of being with Jawad, he had inadvertently led me to a place neither of us had known existed: the site of Mary of Egypt, a place on the Jordan River where the archaeologist Mohammad Waheeb believes thousands of pilgrims came in the Byzantine and Otto-man Eras looking for Mary of Egypt, where she might have taught, where monks, like Zosimas, might have come to see her. It was like that moment when you are walking a labyrinth, and you've come to the farthest out-side circle, as far from the center as you will go and then a few steps later, you are in the center. I thought of Alice Walker's words about bewilderment, "Expect nothing. Live frugally on surprise."

In bewilderment, we cultivate a relationship with un-certainty. Jesus tells us this in the Gospel of John: "The wind blows where it wishes and you hear the sound of it, but do not know where it comes from or where it is going: so is everyone who is born of the Spirit." When we enter into a relationship with the Spirit, we enter into a relationship with the wind. We become attentive to its blowing, but that doesn't mean we know where it came from or where it is going.

Related to an acceptance of uncertainty is a willing-ness to let go. These processes are not in our hands. We do ourselves perhaps the greatest damage when we try to harden ourselves against transformation. It's almost as if we are caterpillars inside the cocoon refusing to become butterflies. We were comfortable creeping along on the ground. We liked it there. This new process is full of un-certainty and risk. We have to become undone in order for it to happen. If you open up a cocoon at the wrong moment, all that will be inside is goo. The poet Mark Nepo writes in *The Exquisite Risk*, "As psychological and spiritual beings, we too can suffer deeply, and sometimes drastically if we don't have enough time to form inwardly." Bewilderment is that time of inward development, when we are becoming more than we were. We are expanding and transforming, becoming available to the next surprise, but it can feel a lot like goo.

This may be why bewilderment is often misunderstood as confusion. When we are confused, we long for clarity, and when we are bewildered, we also long for clarity. But confusion often means that we see the world in a way that is too small and narrow. We get confused because we don't have enough of the picture—the way you can't see the whole puzzle from just one piece. Bewilderment is, by contrast, a process of expansion. More of the world has become available to us. We are moving out of our self-certainties and self-doubt, out of our mental and emotional habits, into a more expansive world, led by God's love.

Bewilderment is less a series of exercises (although I will offer a series of exercises for your experimentation in Part II of this book) and more of an orientation. The poet Fanny Howe calls it "a way of entering the day properly." We know that we don't know. We know that the day holds more than we can possibly experience, and its happenings are outside of our control. This is at the heart of the prayer, "Thy will be done." If we commit to bewilderment, we don't know what God will do with our small lives. The Lord's Prayer, so familiar to many, may actually be the very best practice for bewilderment, as it involves consent to "go beyond your mind," to allow the world and God's presence to be bigger and deeper and wider than you can possibly know or imagine.

Bewilder: Companions and Guides

Baldwin, James. *The Price of the Ticket: Collected Non-Fiction 1948–1985.* Boston: Beacon Press, 1985.

Bucko, Adam. *Let Your Heartbreak Be Your Guide: Lessons in Engaged Contemplation.* Maryknoll, NY: Orbis Books, 2022.

Butcher, Carmen Acevedo. *The Cloud of Unknowing: A Translation.* Boulder, CO: Shambhala, 2018.

Charleston, Steven. *Ladder to the Light: An Indigenous Elder's Meditations on Hope and Courage.* Minneapolis: Broadleaf, 2021.

Fischer, Norman. *Training in Compassion.* Boulder, CO: Shambhala, 2013.

Frykholm, Amy. *Wild Woman: A Footnote, the Desert, and My Search for an Elusive Saint.* Minneapolis: Broadleaf, 2021.

Holmes, Barbara. *Race and the Cosmos: An Invitation to View the World Differently.* Harrisburg, PA: Trinity Press International, 2002.

Neale, Margo, and Lynne Kelly. *First Knowledge Songlines: The Power and Promise.* Port Melbourne, Victoria, Australia: Thames and Hudson, 2020.

Nepo, Mark. *The Exquisite Risk: Daring to Live an Authentic Life.* New York: Harmony Books, 2005.

Starr, Mirabai. *Wild Mercy: Living the Fierce and Tender Wisdom of the Women Mystics.* Boulder, CO: Sounds True, 2019.

Yunkaporta, Tyson. *Sand Talk: How Indigenous Thinking Can Save the World.* New York: HarperOne, 2020.

Invitation Four

Discern

The last of the invitations I offer in this book is the invitation to discern. Discernment declares with some ferocity that even after we've discovered, beheld, and bewildered, we still have work to do. That work in the journey to the wild heart is to discern our own brave next step. Although I've often longed for discernment to be a form of knowing, I've come to perceive it as a form of integration: knowing and unknowing come together.

The approach we are going to take to discernment in this book is a playful one. Without trying to shove discernment through some kind of rigorous process with a guaranteed outcome, we'll integrate what we've learned from the other invitations, and move forward with a sense of openness and possibility.

So we might consider what William Stafford advised: "We are not to try far." Discernment is close at hand. It isn't necessarily some grand thing like a voice telling us to take six months to trek in Tibet. Yes, it might lead to just that kind of thing. We can't guarantee it won't. But it also might feel like one step in a particular direction: one difficult, but necessary conversation, one moment of facing the thing we're most afraid of, one release of a previously held certainty, one gesture, inner or outer, in a new direction. First, we try near. We start with our lives, as we are currently living them, outside our own windows, inside our own bodies and hearts.

When you engage in serious play this way, there are not right and wrong answers. This isn't a pop quiz where after you've discovered, beheld, and bewildered, you suddenly get the answer right or wrong.

One question I've learned to pursue from my spiritual director Sister Therese O'Grady is, "What are God's preferences for my life right now?" This kind of question is packed with gentleness and ordinariness. There aren't absolutes. Sometimes, I swear I've sensed God shrug lovingly and playfully and say, "I don't know. What do you think?"

But at the same time, the practice of discernment means determining what Meister Eckhart calls "going out from what is yours." We look around and we wonder. Is this conversation that I am about to enter into really mine? Or is it someone else's conversation that I have inserted myself into because I am anxious about something? Is this purchase I am about to make for something that is really mine or I am buying this thing (whatever it is) out of a sense of deprivation and lack? Is this task really mine to do or have I stumbled onto someone else's job through my own blindness and carelessness? In the gospels, Jesus teaches a concept of sin that is translated as "trespass," that is taking things, tromping on territory, crossing boundaries to grasp at things that are not really yours. In discernment, we learn to "go out" from what is really ours, so that we avoid trespass, and also find our own narrow way.

What's really yours? This is not something that can be possessed. It is something more like a twinkling, like something that sparkles for you. In the practice of *lectio divina*, a form of divine reading and listening, we practice this discernment through a set of questions: What is alive for you in this text? What has attracted your attention? What is whispering specifically to you? We also practice this in the world outside the text. It's almost like there's a secret highlighter pen, and when we are in the midst of discernment, we can see what is lit up for us.

After we've discerned what's really ours, then we can discern what our own next step might be. There's an ancient practice called *diakresis* that can help us imagine what this might look like. It begins with "really yours" and brings in "not far" repeatedly. For example, I feel a pain in my heart about my niece who is in a relationship that I think is unhealthy. In the practice of *diakresis*, I presume a dialogue with the Spirit, with my own inner guide. I both ask: "Please help my niece," and I ask, "Is there something for me to do here?" There are risks of both over functioning and underfunctioning. Overfunctioning me rushes in to save and fails to respect her own boundaries, needs, and inner dialogue. Underfunctioning me might just shrug and let her go her own way without my interference, not recognizing that there is a role for me to play.

What does *discerning* me do? I lean in and listen. I wait. I ask if there are any specific actions I could take. Write a note of love and encouragement? Invite her for a weekend? I listen for inner yeses and nos. Then I take the best action I can, acknowledging that my own actions will always be imperfect and partial, and the outcome does not depend on me.

While the situation is a serious one, my approach contains elements of play. I experiment. I try. I continue to listen. And I let go.

So here's the ongoing process of discernment as I see it:

> Discern what's mine.
> Go out from it.
> Let go.

A lot of discernment is also recognizing that we don't *do* everything. "Just let God work," Eckhart says, "and be at peace." This may be the most difficult aspect of this invitation: to trust that the work we can see might not be ours to do. The words we can perceive might be someone else's to speak. And meanwhile, in all our awkwardness and confusion and stumbling, God is at work.

I have spent an enormous amount of my life overdoing, overspeaking, overscheduling, over-overing in every area of my life. Not to be too dramatic, but the day of my reckoning came. I had been home from my trek to find Mary of Egypt for a few months, and I'd come home to a difficult situation. My dear friend and the priest of my little church had taken medical leave and was facing a serious cancer diagnosis. I had tried taking up all my ordinary roles in my ordinary life as well as new ones where I saw the community needed help, but I was floundering as I dealt with her illness. It was a cloudy day in March (March 5 to be exact. I won't forget it), during avalanche season in Colorado, when heavy spring snows fall on icy snow from previous, hardened winter storms. I stepped outside before seven a.m. to walk to yoga class, on my to-do list for a busy day. On one side of my street, workers were clearing snow from the sidewalk, so I crossed to the other side of the street. Less than half a block from my house, I slipped on black ice, fell, and broke my wrist.

At the hospital, the radiologist looked at my x-ray and said, "That looks bad." The nurses all echoed her, "That looks bad." The doctor said, "That looks bad. You'll need surgery on that today." The problem was that, to get to the surgery center, I had to cross a mountain pass. The most direct route to the surgery center was blocked due to multiple avalanches. It took an entire day to make my way to the surgery center. So much for my to-do list.

Sitting on the couch with my arm propped up the next day with new metal and a new scar, I heard the Spirit clearly say, "Stop. You have to stop." But I couldn't stop. In my mind, there were so many people dependent on my doing. I was president of the school board. I had a full-time job. My close friend was in the hospital two hours and two mountain passes away, and I had vowed to be there to support her. The little church of which she had been the priest was falling apart. I had a son who was a junior in high school and needed my guidance and my presence. There was no way I could heed that universal call to stop. I was too important. I was also like a speeding train with the brakes gone out. There was no stopping me now.

Within a few weeks, I had added shingles to my broken arm and was lying helpless on the floor of my office, taking a phone call from the superintendent of schools. The police were investigating an accusation of sexual abuse at the preschool. Tears were running down my face, my head felt like it had been placed in a vice, and I had to admit that I could do nothing.

This had become the primary obstacle to my spiritual life: my conviction that my own doing was too important to require discernment. But the truth is, it doesn't all depend on me; it didn't then, at that moment of crisis, and it doesn't now, when the waters are flowing a little more smoothly. "In the innermost source, there I spring out in the Holy Spirit," Eckhart writes, "where there is one life and one being and one work." Our work in discernment is to connect ourselves to that one work and act from the place from which we spring.

In order to accept the invitation to discern and to practice it, I've ended each session in Part II with a space for discernment. This will be your opportunity to write down something you've discovered after you reflect, behold, and bewilder. I've created simple fill-in-the-blanks for discernment for those sessions, like this one:

Because _____, I now discern _____.

You might think this is too rigid and directive for the wild and unruly process of searching, but I encourage you to see it as play, like a mad lib. There are two blanks but countless ways, in discernment, to fill them. Put down the first words that come to mind, perhaps, and then reflect on them later. Or spend a little time in *diakresis*, and then fill in the blanks. Wait and try again. Try filling in the blank ten times instead of one time. Try using your imagination in playful ways or filling in the blank even as a joke.

This isn't about the right answers, so much as it is about finding the still small voice—that weighted clarity—inside you that offers you guidance at every minute of every day, in your very near, on your own journey to the wild heart of contemplative living.

Discern: Companions and Guides

Eckhart, Meister. *Selections from His Essential Writings.* Translation by Edmund Colledge. Edited by Emilie Griffin. San Francisco: HarperCollins, 1981.

Franquemont, Sharon. *You Already Know What to Do.* New York: Penguin, 2000.

Holmes, Barbara. *Crisis Contemplation: Healing the Wounded Village.* Albuquerque, NM: Center for Action and Contemplation, 2021.

Holmes, Barbara. *Walking with Our Ancestors: Contemplation and Activism.* Minneapolis: Fortress, 2024.

Julian of Norwich. *Revelations of Divine Love.* Translated by Elizabeth Spearing. London: Penguin, 1998.

Limón, Ada. *The Carrying.* Minneapolis: Milkweed, 2021.

Nouwen, Henri. *Discernment: Reading the Signs of Daily Life.* New York: HarperOne, 2013.

Palmer, Parker. *Let Your Life Speak.* San Francisco: Jossey-Bass, 2000.

Riley, Cole Arthur. *This Here Flesh: Spirituality, Liberation, and the Stories That Make Us*. New York: Convergent Books, 2023.

Thurman, Howard. *With Head and Heart: The Autobiography of Howard Thurman*. San Diego: Harcourt Brace, 1979.

the sessions

Session One

A DOOR

@

If you have a deep scar, that is a door; if you have an old, old story, that is a door. If you love the sky and the water so much that you almost cannot bear it, that is a door. If you yearn for a deeper life, a full life, a sane life, that is a door.
— CLARISSA PINKOLA ESTÉS

Journey Essentials

- Notebook
- Pen
- Any book that holds a story that is important to you (a children's book, a fairy tale, a Bible story.

You can also refer to the Discover section below for more ideas.)
- Thesaurus (online is fine)
- Timer

This journey toward our own wild heart begins, like all journeys, by crossing a threshold. It begins when we take the first step away from the past and into the future. Folk-lorist Clarissa Pinkola Estés calls this first step a "door" and asks us to think symbolically about where and in what that door might be found. We are looking for a way into our own deeper life, which is a way in and a way out simultaneously. As we walk through this door in this first session, we are seeking what lies beyond the door, what it opens to: a fuller perception of our own very particular and sacred life.

We can begin this session by thinking about the ordinary doors we walk through every day, and then consider the deeper purposes for these ordinary steps. Today, in search of both the internal and external resources to write these pages, I've walked through a number of doors. Literally, these have included the door to my office, the door to the public library, and the door to my kitchen. Symbolically, I've entered portals of conversation; I've sought guidance from people and books; I've knocked on my own interior doors, asking for help from within.

When we go about even the ordinary activities of daily

life, we are seeking many things: home, community, joy, hope, healing, freedom, love. Some of these we've sought by walking through the same door over and over again. Others, we've sought by opening new doors. Sometimes a door opens unexpectedly and decisively for us. Sometimes it closes in the same way. Even if we don't always name what we are looking for when we walk through the doors of our lives, the search is still real. When we name the door—loss, hope, anger, love, beauty, an old story, a scar—we take the first step on an inner journey.

Many years ago, I reached a closed door in my life. I felt stuck, lost, desperate. No matter how much I rattled the knob or pounded on it, I could not open this door. Eventually, I decided that I needed to go deeper inside myself to try to understand why, exactly, this door was closed. Who had closed it? Was it me? Was it God? As I began my internal exploration, I ended up finding another door when I read the words of Julian of Norwich, a 14th century mystic and the first woman to write a book in English. That door was an invitation to a far deeper life than I could have imagined when I stood staring at the closed door between me and what I wanted.

Another person I know began her deep inner journey when she closed the door to a cupboard where she kept the alcohol she was using to numb herself. Closing that door may have been the hardest thing she's ever done, but it was the first step on a transformative journey.

The day in the library when I stumbled on the story about Mary of Egypt, who left everything she knew to find God in the desert, an inner door opened. As I walked through, I allowed a very strange and wild saint to begin to take up space in my inner life and imagination. At first, it was like I could hear her calling out to me from a long way away, and it was many years before I could hear what she was saying.

The story of Mary of Egypt was itself laid out like a series of doors. This curious, wild, and brave woman opened and walked through them all. She kept searching for deeper and deeper doors within herself, even as she walked into wider and wider spaces in the world. Ironically, during her life as a prostitute, the story says she "slept in doorways," as if all doors were closed to her. On her journey, she confronted the closed door at the Church of the Holy Sepulcher, and it allowed her to name her desire for a different life. A door opened from deep inside the world and invited her through it. And later, in the wilderness of Jordan, "a rock gave her shelter" as if every place had become home to her.

This book of invitations came from discoveries I made as I read and explored the old story of Mary of Egypt. Her story started to work on my life, the way rivulets gather to eventually form a creek, and creeks gather to eventually form a river. Sometimes, as I've read this story, I've been the runaway child; sometimes I've been the Mary who sought agency even through her victimization. I've been in the desert, and in the monastery, and in the city. The story continues to open. That's what an old, old story can do. Be a door.

We all have these doors—closed and open, literal and symbolic—ways that we are being guided, beckoned, or invited.

How do we go about identifying these doors? Estés suggests some particular places that we can look: our scars, our loves, our yearnings, and perhaps an old story that we have carried with us.

For this session, we are going to focus on the old story as a door. Pause for a moment to consider what your old story might be. Maybe you know it immediately. Maybe you need to do a little searching. Maybe it is a favorite Bible story that has always stayed with you. Maybe it is a beloved fairy tale that has held a kind of invitation and served as a portal for your wonder. Maybe there is a children's story that you remember.

Scan your bookshelves. Go to the children's section at the library, open the Bible or a text that is sacred to you, and make a brief list of stories that have been meaningful to you throughout your life. If you're stuck, you might try the website fairytalez.com, which contains a rich archive of folktales from around the world. There might be an old story waiting there for you. Folktales contain deep, universal themes, and they can often be rich places to begin your journey.

If you are right now on a pilgrimage or a retreat, chances are there is an old story that compelled you out of your normal life and into the place where you are. What is that story? Let's open this door and begin.

Discover

In your notebook, retell your story in your own words. Don't feel like you have to invent anything. Just tell the story as you would to a child or to someone who has never heard it before. "Once upon a time, there was a boy who ended up in a den of lions." "Once upon a time, there was a man who tried to walk on water, but fell into the waves."

Set a timer for ten minutes and write until the timer goes off, allowing yourself to follow any leads within you that appear during this writing time.

Behold

Once you have your story, written as best you can in your own words, the next invitation is to behold it. Choose a phrase or a passage from the story you've written about.

Once you have the phrase or passage with you, begin the exercise:

Find a quiet place. Move your body into a comfortable position, similar to what you might use to meditate. Perhaps that is sitting in a chair with your back straight and feet flat on the floor or sitting on the floor on a cushion. Set a timer for ten minutes. Next, take a few deep breaths. As you continue to breathe in and out, move your awareness from your breathing to your heartbeat. You may want to move your hand over your heart to feel your heartbeat, and let that quiet rhythm steady you.

Allow your eyes to move over the passage. Read it quietly to yourself or out loud at least three times. Pay attention to the way the words register (or don't) in your mind and heart. If any of them have particular strength or light, write them down. Allow the words to sink in. Remember that your attention will naturally move back and forth from phrase or passage to mingle with your thoughts. This is normal. It doesn't mean you are doing anything wrong. When you realize you've drifted from the phrase, gently guide your attention back to it again.

When the timer goes off, take a few moments to write about your experience, before saying, "Thank you" to whatever emerged.

Bewilder

After beholding, we are going to try to expand our understanding of what is drawing us to this particular story.

Let's try this experiment: Choose one of the words you used in the beholding exercise. Now elaborate and iterate that word in as many forms as possible. Feel free to use a thesaurus for this.

For example, if you choose the word "door," you could write threshold, portal, entryway, gate, aperture, opening, entrance, egress, hatch, way in, hole, rabbit hole, wormhole, gateway, exit, entry-level, prologue, Act I, etc. See how many alternatives you can list. Try to get at least ten. You might also add in metaphors as I just did, that occur to you and feel related.

Next, write out a sentence using that word. For example,

If you love the sky and the water so much that you almost cannot bear it, that is a door.

Now elaborate that sentence, mixing up the nouns and the verbs, and adding in words from your list.

The sky and water I love so much are a threshold. I almost cannot bear it.

I love the sky and the water so much, I almost cannot stand it. But what sky? What water?

I found a door in the sky and the water, but I don't dare walk through it.

There is a portal in the sky, and I want to walk through it.

If I walk through the door in the sky, I will love the water so much I won't be able to endure it.

If I love the water so much, an entrance in the sky will

open, and I almost cannot bear it.

Fill a page this way, letting things get out of hand, if they are willing to. After all this is an invitation to bewilderment. How strange can you let it get? You do not have to make sense to yourself or to anyone else. The point of this exercise is to enter a realm of wordplay so that you can become less attached to your given meanings and imagine new ones or old ones hiding in your own certainty.

See if you can surprise yourself. What do you find when you observe your word or phrase from different angles? Circle one or two sentences from your experiment that you especially like.

Discern

Now take some time in silence. Let the words and ideas and feelings settle around you, like snow falling down in a snow globe. Once you feel a settling, gently ask for help, then breathe into the space you've created. Set a timer again for five minutes and sit quietly, feeling your breath in your body. When the timer goes off, without thinking too much, fill in the sentence below.

I now carry forward _____.

Say thank you and let go.

Session Two

A Time

@

Instructions for living a life:
Pay attention.
Be astonished.
Tell about it.
—FROM "SOMETIMES" BY MARY OLIVER

Journey Essentials

- Notebook
- Pen
- Timer

How many times have you said about the spiritual journey, "I don't have time for this!"? I know, for me, it's a lot. I get so caught up in my daily life that I have trouble reorienting myself to the things that I care about most. Time, for me, is one of my most consistent stumbling blocks. I fear that other people are stealing my time; I imagine that I am wasting my time; I lay awake at night trying to recover lost time.

In this session, we are going to go looking for a time. If you are on a retreat or a pilgrimage, you may have miraculously claimed a time for this important inner work. But even when I am on retreat, my old habits of time can dominate. I think things like: "Am I doing this right? I came all the way here and now I'm wasting time! I feel so tired. All I want to do is sleep. Is that good or bad?" It's usually far more difficult than I imagine to come into the time outside of time for retreat.

My hope is that this session helps all of us claim a time.

I'm inspired in this pursuit of a time by one of the many guides I encountered as I was in search of Mary of Egypt. In Upper Egypt in a place called Nubia, where I was exploring the origins of Mary of Egypt's story, I met Mido. He was a young man who worked as a tour guide. A native to Nubia, he was a kind of visionary in his own right. He spent quite a bit of his life meditating on the golden thread and creating his own brave steps as a result.

One day, Mido took my mother and me to an uninhabited island in the middle of the Nile. It was, essentially, a great big pile of rocks. With all of the other, much more

famous rocks that he had shown us or that we could po-
tentially see (the Obelisk, Philae, Abu Simbel), I was more
than a little curious about why Mido was bringing us here.

"This," he said, with a little smile and a sweep of his
hand, "is Mido Island. This is the place where I come to
think about life, to think about the future of Nubia, to
think about my own future."

Then he gave us an even more important clue. The
best time to come to Mido Island, he said, is at sunset.
When he comes to Mido Island at sunset, he makes a
little fire and brews some coffee. Then as the sun sets, he
looks out over the Nile, over his homeland, and comes
to a deeper understanding of himself and his place in the
bigger world. It felt like an incredible honor to be shown
Mido Island and told about that precious time, like being
invited into a person's inner life.

Later we sat with Mido on the rooftop of his family
home at sunset. We watched the streaks of light fall over the
Nile and its banks. We decided to call sunset "Mido hour,"
the time when this visionary person could best perceive the
golden thread in his life. Mido sparked an understanding
for me of what it means to pay attention and be astonished,
two central actions on the path to inner wildness.

I began to think about my own particular hour—that
time of day when I am most awake to the Spirit's action
and movement in my life. I'm not a night owl like Mido,
so I began to pay special attention to sunrise, instead of

sunset. I found myself seeking out sunrise as a time for my best communion with my inner life. Like Mido, I have rituals associated with this hour of the day. Wherever I am, whatever else I am doing, I find a place where I can look out a window. Then I sit on a cushion for centering prayer. But if I am at home and it really is sunrise, I first watch the light meet the mountains outside my window, that rosy glow that characterizes the sunrise where I live. The light is different every day. It has different colors and interacts with rocks and clouds uniquely depending on the season or the weather or the angle of the sun. After some time on my cushion, I think of Mido as I brew some coffee, pick up my notebook, and write, seeking the golden thread for that day, that moment, that hour.

Discover

What is your hour of the day: the hour when you feel most alive, most available to the deeper forces working on your life, most connected to things greater than yourself? Take a pen and your journal, set a timer for ten minutes, and write about your hour.

Use all your senses to describe this time and the location where this hour usually finds you. What does it smell like? Perhaps it has a taste? What is around you at this time? Consider the feel and textures of the place and time: a scratchy cushion, the fur of the cat, the coldness of the room. What are the sounds, the sights? How does the light fall at this time of day?

And if you find yourself thinking, "I don't have a time of day!" then use these ten minutes just to observe, using your senses, the place and time where you are right now. Pay attention to the light, the sounds, the smells, the textures, and the taste of the now, and record them in your notebook. And, as always, allow this writing to go anywhere it chooses.

Behold

Choose a time of day to behold. Sunset? Sunrise? Midday? Night time? Early morning before dawn? Midafternoon or midmorning? Every time of day has its special elements, feelings, and sensations. The time you choose could be right now, wherever you are when you are reading this.

Find a quiet place, preferably by a window. Begin by moving your body into a comfortable position, similar to what you might use to meditate. Perhaps that is sitting in a chair with your back straight and feet flat on the floor or sitting on the floor on a cushion. Set a timer for ten minutes. Next, take a few deep breaths. As you continue to breathe in and out, move your awareness from your breathing to your heartbeat. You may want to move your hand over your heart to feel your heartbeat, and let that quiet rhythm steady you.

Then watch the light or the dark. Observe its nuances. Notice how it makes you feel. If you are by a window, watch the clouds, the trees, anything that is interacting with the light. Stay like this until the timer rings.

When the timer goes off, take a few moments to write about your experience.

Bewilder

After beholding a time that we've claimed as our own, let's next notice a time that doesn't feel as much like home.[1] At what time of day does your anxiety or depression set in? What time of day often turns to pain or rumination for you? For this bewilder practice, we are going to go deeper into this time of day. Begin by identifying it: Is it on your commute? Is it the middle of the night when you are awakened in ways that are unpleasant? Is it late at night when you have difficulty convincing yourself to lie down and sleep? Or maybe late afternoon when you are hungry and tired and trying to convince yourself to do one more thing. It might take some effort to discover a time of day like this, but once you've identified it, let's go in.

Observe: What does this time of day feel like to you?

---

[1] This practice is adapted from Pedram Shojai, *The Art of Stopping Time: Practical Mindfulness for Busy People* (Emmaus, PA: Rodale, 2017), 11–12.

Is it warm or cold? Can you feel it in your body: the racing heart during merging traffic, the cold letdown when you're still at the computer at ten p.m., the loneliness when you come home after work? Can you attribute a feeling to this time? (Heavy, dull, painful, numbing, fuzzy.) Can you identify a trigger—either in the now or in the past?

At your next opportunity, take your notebook and jot down any of your observations. Allow yourself the opportunity to meet this time as if it were a stranger to whom you were offering hospitality. You aren't trying to change it. You are just trying to meet its discomforts.

Discern

Now take some time in silence. Let the words and ideas and feelings settle around you, like snow falling down in a snow globe. Once you feel a settling, gently ask for help, then breathe into the space you've created. Set a timer again for five minutes and sit quietly, feeling your breath in your body. When the timer goes off, without thinking too much, fill in the sentence below.

Now is the time to _____.

Say thank you and let go.

A place

©

*Reverence the place and learn from what
you see.*

—CYRIL OF ALEXANDRIA

Journey Essentials

- Notebook
- Pen

One of the first lessons of pilgrimage is that wherever
you are is the path. There is no getting there, no final
destination. The way is the destination, many pilgrims
famously have reminded us. This is why people walk the
Camino de Santiago. If the point was to get to the Cathe-

dral of St. James, then you wouldn't bother walking. You'd just drive or take a train there; you'd see the cathedral, take a photograph, and be on your way—wherever that was.

But pilgrimage teaches us a different way of walking. We acknowledge the place where we are as the sacred place, and we acknowledge that we come to be in a place by a slow process.

A lot of the time, we can't see even where we are all that well. Today I biked home from my centering prayer group along a stretch of bike trail that I've been on hundreds of times. I challenged myself to try to really see it. It's not my favorite stretch of trail by any means. The lodgepole pines are pretty scruffy; there aren't many beautiful wild flowers. Mostly you see the motley back ends of other people's houses, and it is entirely uphill, a long, slow slog of a climb.

At first, all I saw was what I thought I would see. Then I heard a rooster crow. I'd never heard a rooster on this stretch of trail. Then I saw a particular kind of native grass that, in midsummer, glows an intense bronze. That bronze is so beautiful if you pause to look at it, it can take your breath away. I was fascinated to see how, in the backyards of the various houses, many people seemed to be building little sanctuaries. There were paintings, a weathered cedar chest, some kind of art made out of aspen branches, and tiny cottages with new windows.

As we go in search of contemplative living, where we

are, and where we think we are, changes. We learn, as Cyril of Alexandria teaches, to reverence the place—any place—and learn from what we see.

When I was in Alexandria, the city where Mary of Egypt lived as a prostitute, I found it pretty hard to see anything that might help me on my quest. There was a lot of sand, some skyscrapers, beaches. When our guide took us to a place whose name in Arabic means "Pile of Rubble," I wasn't expecting much. It was the ruins of the Roman Era in Alexandria, and as I saw the ruins of what lay under the modern city, I decided to practice beholding in this place. I chose the most ordinary place I could in the rubble. There was a series of workshops or maybe ancient shop fronts below the street where I found a place in the shade to sit. Gradually, I was able to begin to imagine the life of a street prostitute in this place, what it meant when the tradition said that she "slept in doorways," how a person might try to survive in a place like this.

The practice of seeing where we are—no matter the place—is a real challenge, and it usually takes time. Again I think of Georges Perec, the French writer, who in the 1970s, set himself up in a cafe in Paris for the exercise he called "attention in place." Perec spent three days in one tiny corner of Paris and recorded everything he observed, especially the ordinary, which he called the "infra-ordinary." "Infra-ordinary" seeing is seeing into the ordinary actions of everyday life and perhaps observing them for the first time. The essay that he wrote about this was called "An Attempt at Exhausting a Place in Paris." Perec challenged himself through these kinds of experiments, because they revealed his own mental habits and the limits of those habits. He also wrote an essay called "Attempt at an Inventory of the Liquid and Solid Food-stuffs Ingurgitated by Me in the Course of the Year Nineteen Hundred and Seventy-Four." Definitely a form of contemplative living! But these experiments also gradually revealed not only Perec's habits, but also the place itself.

A group called the Strother School of Radical Attention follows in Perec's footsteps by taking people out on thirty-minute excursions to jot down observations. When they return to the classroom, they take turns reading one line of their observations one person after the other so that they pay attention not only to their own observations, but also see the place through the eyes of others.

On the journey to the wild heart, we set an intention for being in a place, being present to it, and then we also practice letting our perceptions of it unfold. It's the slow, meandering progress of the pilgrim that we seek in this way that begins wherever we are.

Discover

Start with a blank sheet of paper in your notebook. About halfway down the page, draw a line. Set a timer for ten minutes and begin with the prompt, "This place . . ." Write about a place. Maybe it's a place you pass along your walk or place you drive to; maybe it's a special spot along a riverbed or a labyrinth you go to for times of discernment; maybe it's a favorite coffee shop. Maybe it's just the place where you are. Spend the first half or so of the page (down to the line you've drawn) describing the place physically—smells, sights, textures, sounds—before you begin to write about your experience of it and why you care about it.

Behold

No surprises here. You are going to behold a place. If you can, go to the place that you've just described, and find a comfortable place to sit. Or if you can't go to this place specifically—because it's far away or exists only in your memory—choose a place that is meaningful to you in your current context. Or simply practice wherever you are.

Take a few deep breaths. Say to yourself, "Here I am." Continue to breathe in and out, moving your awareness now from your breathing to focusing on your heartbeat. You may want to move your hand over your heart and let the steady rhythm guide you.

Set a timer and spend the next twenty minutes observing the place. If there are other people, watch them as they come and go. Observe how the place is used and inhabited. Use your senses in this beholding: What do you smell? What do you hear? What are the textures and colors of the space? Are there nonhuman creatures in it? Also observe the intangibles. What does the space feel like? Do you sense a kind of energy in the place—is it frenetic or tranquil? Happily busy and productive? Or is the energy of the space one that feels sacred, somehow set apart from ordinary life?

Observe yourself as well. Do you feel anxious? Do you think people are staring at you, wondering what you are up to? Do you feel at ease? Notice yourself in the space.

When the timer goes off, spend a few minutes jotting down in your notebook what you observed.

Bewilder

I call this exercise "five details." I've practiced it in many places in the world: in my own home, in my own neighborhood, on airplanes, in foreign countries, in hotel rooms. It's an especially good exercise if you are bored or if your senses have become tired.

One of the things that Perec managed to do was to stare at a place until it became strange to him. This is part of what I think he meant by "infra-ordinary." For this exercise in bewilderment, choose a place that is either familiar to you (your own street outside your own window would work) or a place that you think is probably unavailable for surprises. (If you are on a pilgrimage, you might choose the local store or the kitchen of the hostel. It doesn't matter, so long as you don't think of this place as a special one.)

With your notebook in hand, stay in this place until you've observed five details that were unexpected for you. The house sparrows nesting in your neighbor's roofline, someone speaking Hungarian, mustard in tubes, graffiti, the red shoelaces in the shoes of the person sitting across from you. The number of possibilities is, of course, as infinite as the number of places themselves.

Discern

Now take some time in silence. Let the words and ideas and feelings settle around you, like snow falling down in a snow globe. Once you feel a settling, gently ask for help, then breathe into the space you've created. Set a timer again for five minutes and sit quietly, feeling your breath in your body. When the timer goes off, without thinking too much, fill in the sentence below.

Now I am _____.

Say thank you and let go.

Session Four

A companion

◎

It is possible to be wild and kind at the same time. It is possible to be both alone and be loved. I have known this to be true. In others. In me. To be loved. And to also still be alone.

—ANIS MOJGANI

Journey Essentials

- Notebook
- Pen
- Timer
- An icon or an image of a person you consider to be holy (I've done this exercise with traditional icons,

with photographs, with an etching of the Russian rock star Yurii Shevchuk, and with self-portraits by Frida Kahlo, so feel free to think broadly. Choose someone who means something to you.)

- A pencil, a ruler, and a sketch pad or blank sheet of paper
- Any art supplies that are easy for you to have at hand. Maybe water colors, collage materials, colored pencils, scraps of colored paper

I live near the Colorado Trail, and thru-hikers (another kind of pilgrim) often talk about "trail angels," people who appear out of nowhere to provide just what you needed in that moment or companionship on a lonely section of the journey. One woman told me about hiking the Pacific Crest Trail when a man with a taco stand appeared in front of her. She thought it might be an illusion, but the tacos tasted real enough.

I wouldn't have called Mary of Egypt a trail angel exactly because on a lot of my journey in search of her, she seemed to be dancing ahead of me, completely uninterested in being my companion. She was, after all, "one who would not be held." At the same time, by the time I left for my pilgrimage, she'd been my companion in other ways for a long while. An icon of her, written by the icon writer Mary Green, sat on my window sill, and I often looked through her out into the world.

And other trail angels appeared. A young man named Mohammed hiked to the cave of St. Anthony with me—all 1,420 steps—and taught me to count in Arabic as we went. A woman named Anna helped me find the Chapel of Mary of Egypt at the Church of the Holy Sepulchre. Dan from Minnesota helped me interpret the landscape around me. Um Faras fed me shakshuka in a refugee camp outside of Jericho. I could go on and on. Any pilgrim knows the help that appears from unexpected quarters when you've taken the risk and hit the road.

Not too long ago, I was in Agua Prieta, Mexico, on a reporting assignment. I walked into a café, where I was planning to meet someone for an interview. When I entered, there was a man sitting in front of me, and he looked up at me as if he had been waiting for me. I thought he was the man I was supposed to be interviewing, so I asked if he was. "No," he said, "I'm Mickey." Over the next several minutes, he gave me a crucial message about my own life that had nothing whatsoever to do with the assignment that I was on. "Put your heart into your music," he told me. "Always play your music with your heart." I am still not sure how that happened or why tears immediately came to my eyes or why I spent days meditating on this message. Later, upon reflection, I became convinced that Mickey was a trail angel, a companion sent to help me. He was also a human being, on his own journey. For all I know, I was a trail angel for him.

No matter how lonely your own pilgrimage, these companions are around you. In this session, we are going to invite their presence with intention.

Discover

You've brought an image to this session with you. Set the image in front of you and set a timer for ten minutes. Begin by describing the image as you would to someone who couldn't see it; then write about why you brought it and what it means to you. If any memories come up in relation to the image, follow this thread. If you can, perhaps address what this person calls out in you. Who or what is this person encouraging in your becoming? As you write, stay as open as you can to any thread that appears.

Behold

Set your image in front of you again, and move your body into a comfortable position where you can see the image. Set a timer for ten minutes. Next, take a few deep breaths. As you continue to breathe in and out, move your awareness from your breathing to your heartbeat. You may want to move your hand over your heart to feel your heartbeat, and let that quiet rhythm steady you.

Now, bring your attention to the icon or image, asking the icon to draw your attention to what is most needed for you right now. Allow the image to be a companion for you as you grow quiet. Listen to whatever comes up. Whatever comes up is the right thing for you right now. Stay in this position of openness until the timer goes off.

Take a few moments to write about this experience.

Bewilder

Start by using the blank piece of paper you brought to this session and make a window for yourself: measure out a portrait-sized rectangle that feels right to you.

In your journal, write down a few aspects of yourself that are most iconic to you. These might be hobbies, soul traits, passions. Then symbolize them. For example, maybe you see a symbol of a wooden spoon, because you are known to whip up a mean cake. Maybe it's a hammer, because you are known to really go after what you want. Maybe it's a paintbrush or a pen or a book or a tree or a flower. Collect a number of these to use in your self-portrait.

You can use any medium that you want to fill in your self-portrait, but begin with the outline of a head. You might sketch the exact same head in the same position as the one in the icon that you beheld.

Then paint, sketch, draw, collage to fill in this icon with your particular symbols.

This is a difficult assignment. Chances are good that

your inner critic will want to get involved. Just remember that this is a process of discovery. Allow the feelings of awkwardness that come up. Awkwardness is an important sign of bewilderment.

Discern

Now take some time in silence. Let the words and ideas and feelings settle around you, like snow falling down in a snow globe. Once you feel a settling, gently ask for help, then breathe into the space you've created. Set a timer again for five minutes and sit quietly, feeling your breath in your body. When the timer goes off, without thinking too much, fill in the blank.

On this journey, I am becoming _____.

Say thank you and let go.

Session Five

An In-between

Each day bears
some crucial variance.
—BILL CARLY

Journey Essentials

- Notebook
- Pen and pencil; if you have colored pencils, those could also work
- A printout of the human body included below or blank paper for sketching one
- Timer

In texts about ancient pilgrimage, one thing becomes apparent: when pilgrims left their homes to take on the simultaneously metaphoric and tangible road of pilgrimage, they left old rules behind. The rules of the road were not the rules of home. Encounters between strangers, breakdowns of certainties about gender and ethnic roles, new places that demanded new skills—these all effected change. Ancient clerics actually warned about this: pilgrimage is dangerous. Pilgrimage can disrupt our piety, as much as it may enhance it. Some of the church fathers recommended staying at home. It's safer.

When we exit our old lives and stand on the precipice of a new one, desire intensifies. When we're living in our routines of home, we often don't recognize our hungers. We've learned habits of forgetting or stalling or pretending. But when we hit the road on a spiritual journey, desire sneaks in. As we experience new things, we start feeling hungry in ways that we could not have anticipated. It can be unsettling, but the spiritual journey is not designed to make us more comfortable. Even if your version of this journey is taking place in your own home, you might start feeling things stirring inside of you as you pose new questions and try out new practices.

Pilgrimage puts you in a state of vulnerability. You don't know the rules, if there are any, and losing a sense of the rules can be enlivening and awakening, and it can be terrifying and disorienting. Also you might feel incompetent. Maybe you don't speak the language; maybe trying to follow the golden thread feels like groping around in the dark; maybe you end up lost somewhere, literally, and your inner critic has the opportunity to tell you, "Now you've really done it! That's just like you!"

"I don't know how to do this!" might become a refrain, but "I don't know" is one of the pilgrim's most potent friends. "I don't know" is both a sacred place and a sacred moment.

At this point on the journey, we are in-between. We may not know where we are going yet, or we know but we don't know how we are going to get there. In *My Bright Abyss*, the poet Christian Wiman writes that "our minds are constantly trying to bring God down to our level rather than letting God lift us into levels of which we were not previously capable."

As pilgrims, we've set out with just this kind of intention: to no longer be caught in the old "levels," but to allow God to bring us into new levels, to allow God to expand us. This is not a question of intellectual capacities; it's a question of the heart's capacity to love. And if we are going to expand our capacity to love, we have to stay with our unknowing and let it change us. We often try to apply the old rules to the new situation, but that costs us. We sell ourselves short. A better way might be to study the day for its "crucial variance" and let the Spirit lead in the now.

Discover

Take your notebook and a pen, set a timer for ten minutes, and begin with the prompt, "I don't know . . ." Remember that you have the option of repeating the prompt as many times as you need to. You can write, "I don't know" for a whole page or you can explore one particular aspect of your unknowing. The most important thing is to keep your pen moving and let your unknowing take center stage for a few minutes.

Behold

This session's beholding practice involves an exploration that is less tangible. We are going to attempt to behold an emotion or emotions arising inside of us. This can be difficult, like trying to catch a fish with your hands as it moves through the fast-moving stream you stand in. In the *Brief Rule of St. Romuald* (953–1027), the contemplative monk writes to his fellow seekers, "Sit in your cell as in paradise. Put the whole world behind you and forget it. Watch your thoughts like a fisherman watching for fish." Emotion is by its very nature moving, so take some time to observe the movement within the stream, and to accompany yourself as you walk alongside it and feel your way into the next moment and the next.

Find a quiet place. Move your body into a comfortable position, similar to what you might use to meditate. Perhaps that is sitting in a chair with your back straight and feet flat on the floor or sitting on the floor on a cushion. Set a timer for ten minutes. Next, take a few deep breaths. As you continue to breathe in and out, move your awareness from your breathing to your heartbeat. You may want to move your hand over your heart to feel your heartbeat, and let that quiet rhythm steady you.

Now search your mind and body for an emotion. It could be one stimulated by the vulnerability and openness of your seeking or one that is with you now for other reasons. Stay with this emotion. Where is it located in your body? Is it moving or still? Does it have a shape or a texture or remind you of an image? Watch it as best you can, remembering that your ability to perceive it is likely to come and go. Stay in this position of accompaniment until the timer goes off.

Take a few moments to write in your notebook about anything that came up for you.

Bewilder

Everything that has been in this session so far might seem bewildering enough. We've been going deeply into our unknowing. Now we're going to take this exploration a step further.

Here's an outline of a human body:

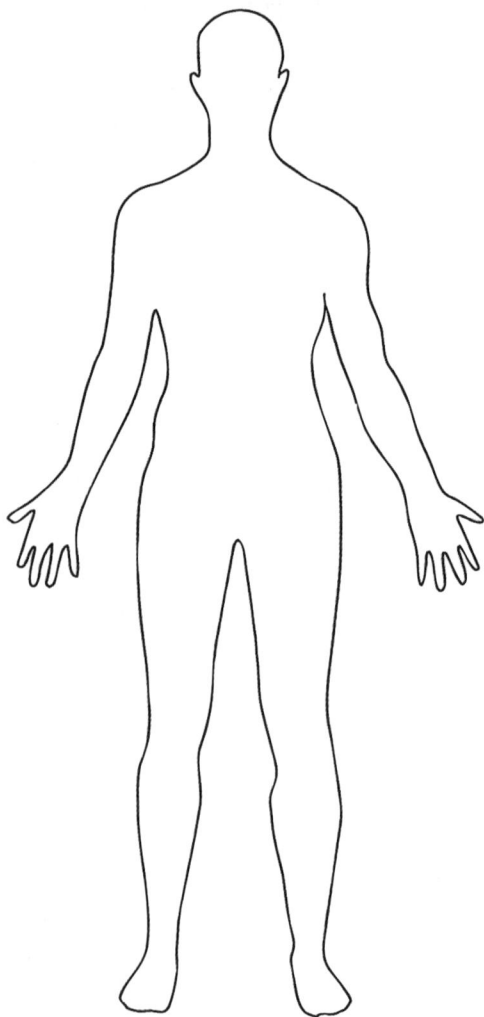

Print this page or simply sketch a rough outline like it on a blank piece of paper. Read through your "I don't know" writing from the Discover section of this session, and as you do, mark any physical or emotional sensations as they appear inside you. You may have to read through it several times, moving back and forth, between your writing and the outline.

Draw symbols within the outline that represent that sensation or emotion. For example, I might draw some dots to represent the tingle along the edge of my left foot, where I often have nerve sensation. It isn't an emotion; it's just a physical feeling that I live with. Every sensation is welcome. For emotions, I might draw a fire in the area of my heart where there is some warmth or a thundercloud in my belly where I have some foreboding. If you feel something, but you don't have a name or a symbol for it, perhaps try a question mark. The things you note do not have to correspond to the writing. The writing is just a prompt to help you perceive what's going on in your inner life.

Do you feel desire? Can you locate it? What about places where your joy lives in your body or a deeply peaceful place, where you feel grounded? You might also discover that you are waiting on the emotion but find it difficult to access. That's natural. You can note those places where something feels foreign, numb, or difficult to access.

Remember to be kind and gentle with yourself as you

do this. We aren't accustomed to paying attention to ourselves this way in our culture. We're used to driving forward from one activity to the next with no perception of how our actions affect our inner life. And remember we're in the "bewilder" invitation. Don't be afraid to let the discomfort or impatience just be what they are. Locate them on the drawing, if you can. Bewilder isn't a "solving" invitation; it's an invitation to notice those things that come up, confusing, maddening, maze-like as they are. You don't have to fix or change anything. If you can, just note it on your sketch.

Discern

Now take some time in silence. Let the words and ideas and feelings settle around you, like snow falling down in a snow globe. Once you feel a settling, gently ask for help, then breathe into the space you've created. Set a timer again for five minutes and sit quietly, feeling your breath in your body. When the timer goes off, without thinking too much, fill in the sentence below.

Because I don't know, I will _____.

Say thank you and let go.

Session Six

An obstacle

Expect nothing. Live frugally on surprise.
—ALICE WALKER

Journey Essentials

- Notebook
- Pen
- A symbol for an obstacle in your search that you've encountered so far. This could be a symbol for an interior obstacle—like a stone for a lack of inner feeling or a symbol for external circumstances like a broken watch for the struggle to find the time to do these exercises.
- A timer

Everything we meet is the path. That's one of the most basic propositions of a pilgrimage—inner or outer. Just as everywhere we are is a sacred place, so everything we meet is an opportunity.

In this session, we are going to be meeting our obstacles. All pilgrims face them. In late winter of this year, I devised a plan to run sections of the Colorado Trail near my house. I did some research and mapped out the sections I thought I could do. Then I sketched out a calendar for my preparation. Although this was a physical goal, it was also a pilgrimage. I've had a complicated relationship to diet and exercise all of my life, and I wanted to approach this physical goal differently than I had in the past. I didn't want there to be anything self-punishing in my attempts. I wanted to enjoy the beauty of nature, the quiet of the trail, and the feeling (I imagined) of freedom in my body. In this way, my desire to run the Colorado Trail was a spiritual desire as well as a physical one. I wanted to be in a different relationship to myself and my environment, to find resources in myself for resilience, to allow the wildness of the trail to change me.

So I started my training. I loved my shoes. I hated the weather. I ran through snow and ice and sleet and wind. I gradually increased my distances as winter turned to spring and spring to summer. Some days my body felt like it weighed 1,000 pounds, and other days I was amazed by the progress I'd made.

And then, after months of gradual training, I ran my first segment of the trail. I hadn't been quite prepared for the sharp ups and downs of the trail or for the rockiness. I came home a little sore, and then that soreness turned into sciatic nerve pain, and for the last three weeks, I've been limping around wondering how to move forward.

How do I face this obstacle? How do I enter into a relationship with it? Likely, as you've attempted this journey, you've faced obstacles yourself. Perhaps there have been limits on the time you've been able to give to your own inner life or you've met your inner resistance in ways that were unexpected. Maybe you've activated your inner critic, and that frenemy has been busy throwing up obstacles in your path.

When I was in search of Mary of Egypt, I caught wind of the fact that there was a chapel dedicated to Mary of Egypt at the Church of the Holy Sepulchre. It seemed imperative that I find this chapel. I tried asking any and every person I could for information, and I got a contra-dictory set of answers. "It's closed." "It's only open once a year." "Ask the Greeks." "Ask the Copts." But I also faced my own embarrassment and uncertainty.

I'm not that good at asking strangers questions. I don't like being told no. It makes me feel like a petulant child.

As I faced this obstacle, I had to find more courage, more hope, more fortitude than I knew I had. I had to turn myself into a stranger again and again and vulnerably admit that I couldn't find a way forward. And gradually, the way opened.

One of the most important moments in Mary's own quest was when she went to the Church of the Holy Sepulchre herself with the pilgrims that she'd followed across the sea and found that everyone but her could enter the church freely to venerate the Holy Cross. For mysterious reasons, she could not. No matter how much she threw herself at this obstacle, it wouldn't budge. The doors wouldn't open for her. This obstacle was of vital importance to her journey.

If she had simply been able to enter the chapel, she never would have discovered her deeper desire to change her life. But at the moment that she confronted it, it felt like the end of the quest.

But for both me and for Mary, the obstacle felt like the end. Instead, it proved a means to a deeper journey.

So we begin to understand that obstacles are simply part of the path. They may in fact *be* the path, if we saw the path from just the right angle. And anyway, we can bring to them the same loving attention that we bring to the journey as a whole, allowing them to offer their strange gifts.

Discover

You've brought a symbol of an obstacle with you to this session. Take your notebook and a pen, set a timer for ten minutes, and write about your symbol and the obstacle that it represents. Note the details of the symbol and allow those details to carry you into reflection on it. Describe emotions that arise as well as physical sensations. Explore all of this on paper, following the symbol's lead, until the timer goes off.

Behold

Set your symbol in front of you again, and move your body into a comfortable position where you can see it. Set a timer for ten minutes. Next, take a few deep breaths. As you continue to breathe in and out, move your awareness from your breathing to your heartbeat. You may want to move your hand over your heart to feel your heartbeat, and let that quiet rhythm steady you.

Now, bring your attention to the symbol, asking the symbol to draw your attention to what is most needed for you right now. Listen to whatever comes up. Whatever comes up is the right thing for you right now. Whatever approach you take, don't try to force anything. Instead, spend time in the presence of your obstacle with curious, nonjudgmental attention. Stay in this position of openness until the timer goes off.

Take a few moments to write about this experience.

Bewilder

Having beheld your obstacle, now let's enter into a conversation with it. Set a timer for ten minutes.

Open your notebook to begin a conversation. You might write, "Hello, obstacle." And then you might feel intensely foolish. Remember that feeling foolish is a good sign of entering into bewilderment. This is a sign that you've entered a realm beyond your own mastery. That's precisely where you want to be. Then maybe you write, "Why are you here?"

The next step is to listen. Don't judge whatever words or phrases emerge. Just write them down. At the moment, they may mean nothing to you, but later they may offer their riches. Continue the dialogue for several minutes, asking and listening for answers. Your obstacle may be silent. Record that too. When you are in the state of active imagination, everything that happens, no matter how tangential it seems in the moment, is important. If you hear song lyrics or remember a favorite biblical passage or something your grandmother once said, this is part of the dialogue.

When the timer goes off, relax and thank your obstacle for its participation.

Discern

Now take some time in silence. Let the words and ideas and feelings settle around you, like snow falling down in a snow globe. Once you feel a settling, gently ask for help, then breathe into the space you've created. Set a timer again for five minutes and sit quietly, feeling your breath in your body. When the timer goes off, without thinking too much, fill in the sentence below.

Because _____, I now know _____.

Say thank you and let go.

Session Seven

A pause

He rested on the seventh day from all His
work which He had done.
—GENESIS 2:2

Journey Essentials

- Nothing

The temptation to make the journey more complicated
than it needs to be is one that I wrestle with daily. I love
tasks, to-do lists, self-help. And when given a task, I love
to elaborate it. Yes, I was that student wanting extra credit.
I was also the student always rushing on to the next thing,
sure that whatever book I had planned to read next was

the best book and whatever assignment I had to do next was the best assignment.

But one key aspect of the spiritual journey is rest. Rest may even be the single most important aspect of the spiritual journey. Rest is how we learn that we are not in charge; we don't own the journey; we don't control it.

So the only thing to do during this session is to rest. Set a timer for sixty minutes if you want to and then let go.

If you are already planning or wondering or imagining how to "do" rest, I get it. There's no one right way. Sit down and do nothing. Wander and do nothing. Lie down and do nothing. You might fall asleep.

You can observe how your mind is always already looking for something to do, wondering when the timer will go off, planning the next move, ready to move on. But you can also release that observation. Whenever doing comes up for you over the next hour, just release it. Smile at yourself and release.

Discover, behold, bewilder, and discern are all likely to make themselves part of this exercise, without any effort on your part. You simply observe yourself as you place yourself in the unusual position of rest without distractions. You might find yourself wandering in a way that resembles the golden thread; you might find your attention drawn to certain places and things and gently observing them; you might find yourself restless and anxious to move on in a way that is a call to bewilderment; and, in the end, new insights and understandings are very likely to come to you as you allow the dust to settle a little and have a look around.

Session Eight

A MAZE

❛

What did you go out into the desert to see?
—MATTHEW 11:7

Journey Essentials

- Notebook
- Pen
- An object from the natural world: a rock, a shell, a leaf, a flower, a fruit
- A labyrinth—life-sized or on paper
- Walking shoes (optional)
- Timer

I don't relish being lost, but I end up lost a lot. I gravitate to imperfect directions, and I often set out with less information than I should have, but I don't recognize the deficiency until it's too late. It's a condition that I've had since I was a child, when I frequently discovered that I had incomplete information only when I was already wandering around not knowing where I was or how to get home. Even in my own mind, I will edit paths I've previously taken, removing crucial information, so that the next time I try to go that exact way, I end up lost. I can't tell exactly what kind of a condition this is. I've called it many things: impatience, arrogance, trust, spatial dyslexia, bad editing, divine leading.

There was one day in Jerusalem when this aspect of myself was in full motion.

I had decided to go to Bethany on the advice of my new friend, Dan Koski, who had urged me to visit a small school for girls run by the Russian Orthodox Church, one that was especially close to his heart. Dan urged me to do this because he wanted me to see "the real desert," not the one that was romantically depicted by the many American spiritual writers who had influenced me. He wanted me to meet Sister Martha, who, he felt, was a real desert saint, living a real desert life on the far side of the Israeli security wall.

I felt that I had, perhaps just barely, enough information to get to Bethany. I had some bus numbers and some instructions. But within an hour of setting out, I was lost. On one side of me was the security wall. On the other side, neighborhoods of East Jerusalem I didn't know anything about.

For some reason, I couldn't find an easy way to solve this problem. Instead, I entered a kind of dreamlike state. I couldn't pull myself back into the realm of good decision making. I walked and walked, imagining that at some point it would become clear what to do. I walked past farms and cemeteries and monasteries. I greeted animals and was met by wandering dogs—who clearly knew what they were about. There were no checkpoints or ways to pass through the security wall, even though I knew Bethany was on the other side.

With all the gates and walls and the smell of animals and no sign of humans, I started to feel like I was in a fairy tale. Eventually, my dream state suggested, I would be met by a witch or a magical creature or at the very least someone who would help me know what to do. It took a long time, but eventually I did. A monk, who spoke a very small amount of English, pointed me back up the hill, the way I'd come.

I hailed a taxi, and I got to Bethany.

On the far side of the experience, I've come to think that my getting lost served a purpose. It took me out of my ego's certainties. It threw me onto the kindness of strangers. It demonstrated, once again, that God can use our faults in our favor, taking us places we need to go even when we are in the midst of bad planning.

There are many kinds of pilgrimage traditions and pilgrimage routes in the world. In some traditions pilgrims traverse a circuit, avoiding a single goal and instead marking numerous shrines or sites along the way. Others have conceived of the ultimate pilgrimage as an endless wandering. Some routes cross dramatic landscapes and hundreds of miles; others cross the wild, interior regions of our souls. In some Indigenous traditions, spiritual paths are marked by their nonlinear nature, while the path of illness or insanity is marked by a straight line. As Indigenous scholar and activist Tyson Yunkaporta writes in his book *Sand Talk*, "We don't have a word for nonlinear in our languages because nobody would consider traveling, thinking, or talking in a straight line in the first place. The winding path is just how a path is, and therefore it needs no name."

On our spiritual paths, we can easily underestimate the power of getting lost. We transport our goal-oriented mind-set into the experience. But our tradition speaks again and again to the importance of the wilderness and of wandering in the wilderness. It's in our lostness that we can be found by something greater than ourselves and that we can get caught up in a story we didn't even know we were in—and that is different, and larger and more significant than the story we thought we were telling.

Discover

Can you answer Jesus's question? You've come this far into the desert on this journey. Do you know now what you've come to the desert to see? Set your timer for ten minutes, and begin with the prompt, "I think I came looking for . . ." Even if you don't have answers, reflect on this question in your notebook until the timer goes off, allowing your pen to do the wandering for you, allowing yourself to walk into dead ends and along walls that seem to be blocking your view. Perhaps, as you reach a dead end, start again with the phrase, "I think I came looking for . . ."

Behold

"Attention consists of suspending our thought, leaving it detached, empty, and ready to be penetrated by the object," writes Simone Weil. "Neutral, ready, susceptible to now," William Stafford says, describing the posture.

Set your object in front of you, and move your body into a comfortable position where you can see it. Set a timer for ten minutes. Next, take a few deep breaths. As you continue to breathe in and out, move your awareness from your breathing to your heartbeat. You may want to move your hand over your heart to feel your heartbeat, and let that quiet rhythm steady you.

Now bring your attention to your object. Use your senses to perceive the object. Listen to whatever comes up. Don't try to force anything. Instead, spend time in the presence of your object with curious, nonjudgmental attention. Stay in this position of openness until the timer goes off, allowing yourself to be led by your object.

Take a few moments to write about this experience.

Bewilder

For this invitation to bewilder, we will practice walking nonlinear paths. Find a labyrinth (labyrinthlocator.org) near you or simply use the one that I have included here and "walk" it using your fingers.

At the beginning of your labyrinth walk, put the object that you used during the behold exercise in your hand or in your pocket. Say out loud one sentence from the writing that you did during the invitation to discover. "I think I am looking for . . ." Then begin to walk. Find a pace that is slower than your natural pace and observe whatever comes up for you as you walk. Don't feel you need to focus on your statement. Simply walk in the present moment. When you reach the center of the labyrinth, place your object there as an offering. Repeat your statement, "I think I am looking for . . ." Then slowly walk out. When you return, spend a few minutes journaling about the experience.

Discern

Now take some time in silence. Let the words and ideas and feelings settle around you, like snow falling down in a snow globe. Once you feel a settling, gently ask for help, then breathe into the space you've created. Set a timer again for five minutes and sit quietly, feeling your breath in your body. When the timer goes off, without thinking too much, fill in the sentence below.

At the center of the labyrinth, I knew _____.

Session Nine

A Moment

The present moment is always full of infinite treasure; it contains far more than you have the capacity to hold. Faith is the measure: what you find in the present moment will be according to your faith. Love is the measure: the more your heart loves, the more it desires, and the more it desires, the more it finds.

—JEAN-PIERRE DE CAUSSADE

Journey Essentials

- Notebook
- Pen
- Timer

- If you like, some sensory materials: a bell, a candle, a feather, a piece of chocolate

For this session, we are going to look for treasure in the present moment. Not some other time and some other place. Not in the future or in the past, but right here, right now. This is the place and the time we are always rushing past.

But everything we've practiced so far in this journey leads us to no other place or time than here and now.

Right now and right here for me, I am sitting at a desk that is too messy for my liking, and my inclination is to pause and clean it off before I begin. Suddenly my fingers itch to touch the objects on my desk, not because I want to pay attention to them, but because I want to improve on the present moment. I'd much rather put away those scissors and take that plate to the kitchen and reorganize all the books I've piled up. Maybe now isn't the time after all. Maybe the present moment isn't the measure after all.

I return to the present moment again, scissors and plate and books untouched. Doubts and jumpiness here with me, within me.

My window faces west, and so the light coming in this morning is muted, soft. I can still taste the breakfast I just ate and smell the coffee that was brewed. Outside,

Terry, who works for the city maintenance department, is weed-whacking under the picnic tables at the park. Terry loves this park, and he seems to find something to do here every day. He smooths the gravel, he mows the grass, he fixes up the bathrooms. He is wearing a bright yellow vest and big floppy hat. Even though I don't love the machines that Terry brings with him, I do love how he loves this park. His care for it speaks to me in the present moment.

Is this the kind of love that Jean-Pierre de Caussade speaks of when he says that we reach through the present moment via faith, love, and desire? Is Terry part of the infinite riches offered to me? He must be.

My search unfolds just like this—one moment at a time. Terry is the golden thread. So is that plate with the skim of breakfast on it, and these books that represent so much of what I've been searching for. I don't know about the scissors, but I remember Stafford saying, so emphatically, "every thread!" I notice the aspen tree outside my window in full summer clothes. I notice the now-empty bird feeder.

In a poem by Caribbean poet Derek Walcott called "Love After Love," the poet invites you, as if you were a stranger, into your own house, to sit down at your own table, and to "feast on your life." "Give back your heart to itself," he writes.

As I sit here in this present moment, I begin, ever so slowly and gently, as if being nudged by a feather, to enter my own life once again.

Discover

Take your notebook and a pen. Set your timer for ten minutes. Describe your present moment. The prompt can be, "I am . . ." Where are you? What is the light like in the place where you are? What is the quality of the air? What do you see from where you sit? What do you feel like in this moment? What is the quality of your inner life? What are you sitting on? What are the objects near at hand? What season is it? What hour of the day or night is it?

Allow your pen to move freely. If it moves from the present moment into story or thought, follow it. And if you find yourself at a dead end, just return to the present moment, the quality of the air, what you see in front of you, etc.

Behold

For this invitation, we are simply going to behold the present moment. If you feel like gathering some props around you—things that you can hear, see, smell, touch— feel free. But you can also just accept the present moment as it is. Begin by moving your body into a comfortable position, similar to what you might use to meditate. Perhaps that is sitting in a chair with your back straight and feet flat on the floor or sitting on the floor on a cushion. Set a timer for ten minutes. Next, take a few deep breaths. As you continue to breathe in and out, move your awareness from your breathing to your heartbeat. You may want to move your hand over your heart to feel your heartbeat, and let that quiet rhythm steady you.

Go through your five senses systematically: What do you hear? See? Smell? Taste? Touch? As you experience each sense, also try to sense the inner stirrings that that particular scent, sound, sight, taste makes within you. Do you have an emotional response as well as a physical one? Do you have thoughts that come up, memories, perceptions? Does an inner critic start talking or an inner angel?

Behold the present moment until the timer goes off. You might take some time to write about your responses and discoveries, how it feels to be in the present moment, present surroundings, present to the sensations of this moment.

Bewilder

Although hope to receive insight, wisdom, or an answer to a question is often a part of a pilgrimage, it is also common for pilgrims to give alms, or to perform acts of reverence or offer prayers at a sacred site. Throughout history, acts performed at pilgrimage sites have included kissing the place or object, reciting scripture, saying a prayer, reenacting a scene, singing, offering a blessing, or leaving a token.

If you are reading this in the American context, you may very well not be comfortable with many religious gestures. We've been trained to be spectators in the realm of religion, not participants.

So even if it feels awkward or uncomfortable, attempt one of these practices now. Find a small gift to offer to the present moment. Maybe it is a song, an object, a flower, a rock, a gesture, a kiss.

In both quests and life, it can be easy to get caught up in what we hope to receive, whether that's from other people, from God, or from our spiritual tradition. But these various acts of devotion remind us of the power of giving—how offering up prayer or a devotion—can transform us in ways receiving cannot.

Discern

Now take some time in silence. Let the words and ideas and feelings settle around you, like snow falling down in a snow globe. Once you feel a settling, gently ask for help, then breathe into the space you've created. Set a timer again for five minutes and sit quietly, feeling your breath in your body. When the timer goes off, without thinking too much, fill in the sentence below.

Now_____.

Say thank you and let go.

Session Ten

A Dragonfly

The desert is not a place; it's a way.
—John Chryssavgis

Journey Essentials

- Journal
- Pen
- Timer
- A symbol, drawing, icon, or other metaphoric representation of your journey so far

In his book *Sand Talk*, aboriginal philosopher Tyson Yunkaporta writes, "Metaphors are the language of the spirit." He explains that we live in both spiritual and material realms simultaneously, but these two realms don't always share the same language or the same experience. Metaphors help us bridge the gap between the two. "They go around," he says, "top and bottom, because you need to close the feedback loop." Abstract information received in the spiritual realm needs a concrete form to be incorporated into your physical life, and the form that can very often take is metaphor.

Every metaphor is like a tiny creation event in your brain. It connects things that were previously unconnected, sending little waves of pleasure and sparks of newness into our human experience.

During the last days that I spent searching for Mary of Egypt, I encountered another young guide named Monther whose job it was to take me through a place called the Wadi Hasa, the closest I could come to what the literature about Mary of Egypt called "the deeper desert."

Monther loved Wadi Hasa. "It is a magical place," he told us. And his spirit of play was present everywhere. He immediately waded into the stream when we reached the starting point of our hike. He laughed, joked, and talked openheartedly about his life, as he led us deeper and deeper into the canyon. Wadi Hasa was his happy place, and he all but danced his way through our hike.

He had found Wadi Hasa the hard way: through a series of struggles with himself, his family, and the meaning and purpose of his life. He told us about attempting to follow the path of his uncle, a judge much admired by his family. He told us about a terrible day when ISIS tried to recruit him. He told us about being a disappointment to his parents, trying and flailing his way through university.

The first time he went out in the wilderness, he told us, he brought with him an enormous hookah. His friends laughed, "What do you think you are going to do with that thing?" It took him some time to be in the wilderness on its own terms, to travel lightly, to trust the path in front of him.

Eventually, he said, the wilderness taught him everything he needed to know. Now he goes into the natural world in search of healing, and he has started taking other young people—including children who have fled the war in Syria—with him, knowing that nature has the power to heal them.

As we walked along, he pointed out strange, grasshopper-like insects that were clinging to the rocks. They looked like they were poised and ready to jump. "Go ahead," he said. "You can touch it. It's not alive."

"Really?" I said, a little distrustfully. I picked the papery body from the rock.

"It's the . . . how do you say it? Evolution of the dragonfly? The back is open, and the dragonfly flies out. Not evolution. Life cycle. It is like a butterfly, when it is a caterpillar and then it becomes a . . ."

"Cocoon."

"Cocoon. That is the cocoon of the dragonfly."

I stared at the beautiful, but empty, body on my palm. Around us, we saw many dragonflies in flight, and everywhere we looked on these rocks were shells, eerily poised, "as if" alive.

I started to understand this dragonfly shell as a metaphor for my journey. As I'd walked along, I'd been discarding my old life, and trying to comprehend the new. I was walking into the fragile possibilities of a life I couldn't yet see, with Mary of Egypt as my guide. I was preparing to take flight into a wider, deeper, and wilder life than I could have imagined when I set out. While there was no way for me to pick up a dragonfly shell and carry it home with me, I could still hold on to it, as a metaphor, and allow it to speak to me of the bridge between the spiritual world and my unfolding physical life.

Metaphors are powerful bridges—they carry us to new understandings and new ways of claiming our lives and our journeys. And they are like prisms; you can walk around and around them and see new things. They shift and they change with perspective and the passage of time.

Discover

At the beginning of this journey together, Christina Pinkola Estés told us there was a door that we could find into a "deeper life, a full life, a sane life." For this invitation, take your notebook and a pen. Set your timer for ten minutes and spend some time reflecting on what that life is for you. What is a deeper life, a full life? What is a sane life? How do you imagine it? What are its markers? What in your life now works against that full life? Write freely. Take more time if you need it.

Behold

For this invitation, we are going to behold the symbol of your journey that you brought with you. Set your symbol in front of you, and move your body into a comfortable position where you can see it. Set a timer for ten minutes. Next, take a few deep breaths. As you continue to breathe in and out, move your awareness from your breathing to your heartbeat. You may want to move your hand over your heart to feel your heartbeat, and let that quiet rhythm steady you.

Now bring your attention to your symbol. Use your senses to perceive the object. Listen to whatever comes up. Don't try to force anything. Instead, spend time in the presence of your symbol with curious, nonjudgmental attention. Stay in this position of openness until the timer goes off, allowing yourself to be led by your symbol.

You may want to take a few minutes to write about this experience in your notebook.

Bewilder

We are going to practice making metaphors. You don't have to be any good at it. If I asked you to pick up a trumpet right now and start playing and you weren't already a trumpet player, how would it sound? Not great, but novel, right? That's the sound of you playing the trumpet, a sound never before heard on earth. A lot of us like doing things we're good at because it makes us feel safe, but bewilderment—the path of the spirit, the path of Jesus—asks us for another way. We stay in our discomfort; we allow ourselves the experience of *metanoia*.

So place your symbol once again in front of you. Take a piece of paper and a pen and start playing with metaphors. If you like, you can ease in with similes. Sometimes they make an easier path for the mind. *This dragonfly is like a jewel all lit up from the inside. It's like the pearl in my grandmother's necklace. It's like the neon sign that says Jesus Saves on that street in my hometown that I no longer remember the name of.*

Then, moving as freely and loosely as you can, move on to metaphor: *This dragonfly is my mother's name, if she'd known her name. This dragonfly is Monther, finding his way through the wilderness. This dragonfly is a high priestess in the Temple of Life. This dragonfly is my own new life, where I am going to eat more insects and fly more often.*

Kay Ryan has written about how Emily Dickinson's poetry is "buoyed by nonsense." In a sense, that's what bewilderment is. You allow yourself the possibility of entering into a realm where no meaning might be made at all, and so you find new meanings that can and will "buoy" you as you break out of old certainties.

Fill a page with these metaphors, letting them get as nonsensical as you like. When you have a page full, read back over it and circle your one or two favorites.

Discern

Now take some time in silence. Let the words and ideas and feelings settle around you, like snow falling down in a snow globe. Once you feel a settling, gently ask for help, then breathe into the space you've created. Set a timer again for five minutes and sit quietly, feeling your breath in your body. When the timer goes off, without thinking too much, fill in the sentence below.

Because _____, I now discern_____.

Say thank you and let go.

journeying on

There is a place near my house where I often go, in all seasons, and all kinds of weather. To get there you first have to cross a landscape of devastation, where there used to be a smelter that churned out and left a black substance that isn't soil. There's so much of it that it has created a whole plateau within the landscape. Constant erosion creates caves within the blackness; the occasional plant makes its way through the crevices, but otherwise nothing grows. It's an eerie place—this abandoned remnant of the mining district. And even outside the expanse of black, hard, shiny ground, you can feel the poverty of the soil. Second growth lodgepole pine is the most common tree. Sage covers any open expanse, offering the soil much needed tonic.

But on the edge of this devastation, there is an aspen grove. You can see it at some distance, the white bark

rising up distinctively, markedly different from everything around it. In every season, the bark sets this place
apart, and the leaves go through glorious cycles from fat,
almost red nibs to tender green to rippling full green to
gold-fringed to full gold to stark, brittle brown. In every
season, entering the aspen grove via a dirt path feels like
you are entering a sanctuary. What was loud becomes
soft. What needed to be said falls into silence. The route
through the aspen grove descends to a creek bed that
opens into a meadow surrounded by willows and currant
bushes, and then becomes an aspen grove again as you
trace the creek up to a place I call The Crossing.

The Crossing is created by a creek called Evans Gulch
Creek. It starts with rills high up in the Mosquito Range
to the east of Leadville, the old mining town where I live.
Snowmelt trickles to form a creek that then diverges—one
rivulet heading into reservoirs that host the town's water
and one that continues along through The Crossing,
edging the former smelter toward the headwaters of the
Arkansas River.

The Crossing is an ordinary place that you would probably pass by without any particular notice. A path runs
down from the paved bike trail and runs into the creek;
other paths come up from the creek and continue into
the forest. This is all privately owned land, although the
owners spend little time on it, and some may not even
know that they own it—such is the legacy of an aban-

doned mining area. Local people ski, bike, hike, walk their dogs, make trails, snowmobile through this place. I for one feel a constant anxiety that it will be "discovered" by developers, and its fragile reconstitution in the decades after mining will be destroyed by new obsessions.

I remember the first time I was taken to this place. It was fall and the aspens were turning gold. A friend was taking a small group on a run. I was anxious about keeping up with these athletic women who had ambitious plans for their running. Some were planning ten-mile runs, some fifty, some one hundred. I was hoping that the five miles we were doing right then wouldn't kill me.

But Kendra, in the lead, guided us toward this aspen grove, and as we entered, the chatter of the group died away. My ambitions and comparisons became meaningless in front of the beauty that surrounded me. It was like entering the hush of a cathedral—patterns of gold above us, the blue sky, gold under our feet, a creek gently flowing by. Surrounded on all sides by old mining ruins, it was an astonishing place of beauty and rest.

I started to come to this place all the time. In early spring, I sat on the banks of the creek and waited for birdsong. I watched for the first fuzzies on the willows to appear. I picked currants, juniper berries, and rose hips, and I crushed sage leaves in my palm. I returned again and again, like a ritual, like a mass, like a little visit to my soul and to something larger than my soul.

The Crossing itself is an ever-changing cascade of water, shaped by seasons and rainfall and snowfall and the lack thereof. It's a place of discovery, beholding, bewildering, and discernment. I go there to reconnect with the deep life I am always in search of. To me, there's a kind of crossing of heaven and earth here: the human and the more-than-human, the physical and the spiritual. Somehow The Crossing has posed to me the essential questions of my life and helped me locate them inside a practice. The Crossing has been a way that the ends of the golden thread I found while in search of Mary of Egypt continue. It enters my daily life and brings me into engagement with something both deep within and outside myself.

While the four invitations of this book arose from the necessities of pilgrimage in my search for Mary of Egypt, it wasn't until I returned that these invitations took a sustainable form in my life. And these practices are meant for you to extend to places like The Crossing. By now, you probably know that I will suggest that these places are both interior and exterior landscapes, places for introverted pilgrimage and extroverted mysticism. I hope you have found—through your explorations—a place like The Crossing in your own everyday life. Perhaps it is simply a view out a window or a corner in your own kitchen. Perhaps it's a place inside you where your heart can rest. Even though we began these practices in special, perhaps set-apart times and places, they are meant to seep out into everyday life and take hold there.

Once we've gone through periods of transformation in our lives, we then go through periods of translation, where the newness we've found gradually permeates every area of our lives and remakes them. This is contemplative living, and it is a process that can take years. There's nothing immediate about it. The unfolding that's involved is slow, careful, unhurried, and deeply loving. God is always working toward our inner freedom—toward our wild heart.

Daily life with its challenges, encounters, and ceaseless invitations is also a door. It's the only place, after all, where we'll eventually find "a deeper life, a full life, a sane life."

acknowledgments

Thank you to Lil Copan, as she has been several times in my life a fearless, creative, and generous editor. And thank you to the team at Orbis Books for the care they've put into this book.

Thank you to Amie Adams, who helped me create an early draft of these exercises and helped me see what I couldn't see alone.

Thank you to Melissa Earley for teaching me about the golden thread and helping me practice with it.

Thank you to Emma Cary, Susan Fishman, Karen Johnson, Lisa Morton, Marty Remsen, and Sarah Strehle, who have shown me the power of a creative community.

Thank you to Kira Cunningham, Ali Lufkin, and Kirsten Sampera—companions of the journey and saints of my little life.

Thank you to my centering prayer group for giving me a place to practice.

Thank you to Peter and Sam, whose love and forbearance continue to surprise and delight me.